03/18
25.00

MANAGING
THE MYTHS OF
HEALTH CARE

BRIDGING THE SEPARATIONS
BETWEEN CARE, CURE, CONTROL,
AND COMMUNITY

HENRY MINTZBERG

BK

Berrett–Koehler Publishers, Inc.
a BK Business book

Berrett-Koehler Publishers, inc.
1333 Broadway, Suite 1000
Oakland, CA 94612-1921
Tel: (510) 817-2277   Fax: (510) 817-2278   www.bkconnection.com

Ordering Information

Quantity sales. Special discounts are available on quantity purchases by corporations, associations, and others. For details, contact the "Special Sales Department" at the Berrett-Koehler address above.

Individual sales. Berrett-Koehler publications are available through most bookstores. They can also be ordered directly from Berrett-Koehler:
Tel: (800) 929-2929; Fax: (802) 864-7626; www.bkconnection.com

Orders for college textbook/course adoption use. Please contact Berrett-Koehler: Tel: (800) 929-2929; Fax: (802) 864-7626.

Orders by U.S. trade bookstores and wholesalers. Please contact
Ingram Publisher Services, Tel: (800) 509-4887; Fax: (800) 838-1149;
E-mail: customer.service@ingrampublisherservices.com;
or visit www.ingrampublisherservices.com/Ordering for details about electronic ordering.

Berrett-Koehler and the BK logo are registered trademarks of Berrett-Koehler Publishers, Inc.

Printed in the United States of America

Berrett-Koehler books are printed on long-lasting acid-free paper. When it is available, we choose paper that has been manufactured by environmentally responsible processes. These may include using trees grown in sustainable forests, incorporating recycled paper, minimizing chlorine in bleaching, or recycling the energy produced at the paper mill.

Production Management: Michael Bass Associates
Cover/Jacket Designer: Dan Tesser / Studio Carnelian

Library of Congress Cataloging-in-Publication Data
Names: Mintzberg, Henry, author.
Title: Managing the myths of health care : bridging the separations between care, cure, control, and community / Henry Mintzberg.
Description: First edition. | Oakland, CA : Berrett-Koehler Publishers,Inc., [2017]
Identifiers: LCCN 2016059033 | ISBN 9781626569058 (pbk.)
Subjects: LCSH: Health services administration. | Health policy. | Health planning.
Classification: LCC RA971 .M534 2017 | DDC 362.1068—dc23
LC record available at https://lccn.loc.gov/2016059033

First Edition

22 21 20 19 18 17   10 9 8 7 6 5 4 3 2 1

CONTENTS

Contents

Contents

——— PART II: ORGANIZING ———

Contents

PART III: REFRAMING

Contents

Contents

EXHIBITS

BOXES

FIGURES

OVERVIEW

THIS BOOK IN BRIEF

This book is written for everyone engaged in health care: clinical and other professionals, managers, and policy makers, to be sure, but also the rest of us, as people beyond "patients." (When I exercise to care for my health, am I a patient?)

I have written this book in an easy style, to make it accessible to specialists and laypeople alike. All of us need to better understand the strengths and shortcomings of this system called health care. We can start by asking ourselves if the labels *system* and *health care* really describe what constitutes mostly a collection of treatments for diseases.

All over the world, people rail on about the failings of their health care. Yet we are living longer, thanks to the many advances in these treatments. In other words, where it focuses its attention, this field is succeeding, not failing, sometimes astonishingly. But it is doing so expensively, and we don't want to pay for it. So the administrators of our health care, in governments and insurance companies alike, have been intervening to fix it, mostly by cutting costs. And here is where we find a good deal of the failure.

Is management, therefore, the problem? Many health care professionals believe so. I don't. Health care cannot function without management, but it can certainly function without a form of management that has become too common. I call it *remote-control* management because it is detached from the operations yet determined to control them. It works badly even in business, from where it has come. In health care, it reorganizes relentlessly, measures like mad, promotes a heroic form of leadership, favors competition where there is the need for cooperation, and pretends that this *calling* should be managed like a business. The more of all this we get, the more dysfunctional health care becomes.

All of this is the subject of Part I of this book, called "Myths," to open up perspectives. As you can see, it is somewhat polemical in nature, although most of the conclusions are backed up by evidence and illustrations from experience, a number of these in the supporting footnotes.

Part II, called "Organizing," serves as a bridge between Parts I and III, by considering how we organize in general and for health care in particular. In general, we differentiate work into component parts and then integrate these parts into unified wholes. In health care, however, there tends to be a lot more differentiating than integrating, and this has encouraged all sorts of excessive separations: "consulting" physicians who barely talk with each other; a preoccupation with evidence at the expense of experience; the researching of cures for diseases while failing to investigate their causes; persons reduced to patients and communities reduced to populations. And in the administration of health care, there are those walls and floors that separate managers from each other and from the professionals.

Behind all this lies a particular form of organizing that dominates the delivery of health care services. To understand it, turn on its head much of what you know about conventional organizing. For example, here strategy and leadership do not so much descend from some metaphorical "top" as emerge from the base; bigger is not inevitably better; and many of the most successful institutions are neither private nor public.

This *professional* form of organizing is the source of health care's great strength as well as its debilitating weakness. In its administration as in its operations, it categorizes whatever it can, in order to apply standardized practices whose results can be measured. When the categories fit, this works wonderfully well. The physician diagnoses appendicitis and operates; the government or insurance company ticks the appropriate box and pays. But what happens when the fit fails? For example, who cares for the patient who falls between the categories, say, with some form of autoimmune illness that medicine has yet to prototype? Or how about the patient who fits the category but is ignored as a person, and so does not respond adequately to the treatment? Even more damaging can be the misfit between managers and professionals, as they pass each other like ships in the night, the managers in their hierarchy of authority, the professionals in their hierarchy of status.

This takes us to Part III of the book, called "Reframing," about how to achieve the necessary integration, so that heath care can function more like the system it is thought to be. Its management can be reframed as engagement rather than detachment—or, if you like, as caring more than curing. (Dare I say, like nursing more than medicine?) And it can be seen as distributed beyond just those people called managers. Thus strategies, rather than descending immaculately conceived from some metaphorical top, can be seen to emerge from the base as professionals in the operations learn their way to new forms of care and cure.

The organization of health care can be reframed by encouraging collaboration to transcend competition, culture to transcend control, and what we shall be calling "communityship" to transcend leadership. More broadly, the raging battles over public sector versus private sector health care can be reframed with the recognition that the best of our professional services are often delivered by community institutions, in another sector altogether, which we shall be calling *plural*.

Overall, care, cure, control, and community have to collaborate, within the health care institutions and across them, to deliver quantity, quality, and equality simultaneously. To introduce a metaphor that you will read about again, a cow works as a system: all its parts function harmoniously together. So why can't health care?

YET AGAIN?

So here comes yet another outsider who thinks he can help resolve the confusing state of management in health care. Is this book any different?

I hope so. For one thing, I am critical of outsiders who I believe have often made things worse, not better. (Does it take one to know one?) For another, I advocate for the elevation of insiders who know health care on the ground, in their hearts and souls. Administrative intervention alone will not resolve the problems of this field. There are no management problems in health care, separate from medical problems or nursing problems or prevention problems.

In preparing this book, I have consulted colleagues who know better than I do, ones who have devoted their careers to health care. I may have misunderstood some of their advice, so please be prepared to discount some of what you read here, although what that is I cannot say (or else I would have changed it). But don't be too quick to dismiss anything that seems outrageous, because questionable ideas can sometime provoke useful learning.

Like many of these outsiders, my field is management, although health care managers and their organizations have figured prominently in my research.[1] Where these outsiders and I part company is in my view of management and leadership. As you will see, I consider leadership the problem more than the solution, especially when it is promoted as being superior to plain old managing.

Likewise, I question conventional ways of developing managers, MBA programs and the like included. Mostly they teach an analytical approach to a job that is primarily practiced as craft with art. Moreover, I am suspicious of measurement too, at least as a panacea, and I believe that strategic planning is an oxymoron: strategies have to be learned on the ground, not deemed in offices.

MANAGEMENT? or management?

Many professionals in health care see management as the enemy. How often have you heard a hospital physician dismissing a colleague who has moved into management as no longer a physician? I understand where these concerns are coming from: all those administrative forms to fill out, all that jerking around by the managerial flavor of the month, etc. "Why can't we just be left alone?" Because being left alone is a part of the problem.

---

[1] My doctoral thesis on the *Nature of Managerial Work* (Mintzberg, 1973) included the head of the Massachusetts General Hospital among the five chief executives I observed, while my more recent research on this subject (Mintzberg, 2009, 2013; see also 1994 and 2001) has included seven health care managers of all sorts among the 29 managers I observed. I have also published an article about a month I spent on and off studying the management problems of a teaching hospital (Mintzberg, 1997). In my writings on forms of organizations (Mintzberg, 1979, 1983, 1989), the "professional organization" (or "professional bureaucracy") has attracted particular attention in the field of health care. Other papers of mine in the field include Glouberman and Mintzberg (Parts I and II, 2001) on a framework about care, cure, control, and community in health care, and Mintzberg (2006) on the "Patent Nonsense" of the pharmaceutical industry. See also Mintzberg (2012) for an earlier summary of this book.

My health and yours is not about a collection of disconnected interventions; it has to be dealt with systemically, in the clinics and the offices together. Professionals, too, must be engaged, with more than their professions.

In 1977, Albert Shapero wrote an article that compared MANAGEMENT with management. MANAGEMENT, essentially the remote-control type, tries to achieve this integration cerebrally, analytically. But who ever got near synthesis by relying on analysis? What we need therefore—within our institutions and across the so-called system of health care—is plain old managing, as a natural human practice, rooted in craft and art (as described in my book *Simply Managing*, 2013).

From a systems perspective, the narrow knowledge of self-serving professionals is hardly better than the broad ignorance of disconnected managers. (Throughout the book, key sentences are highlighted in **boldface** type.) This field needs professionals and managers who see past their jobs, outside their specialties, and beyond their institutions, to the needs of everyone's health.

A FEW CAUTIONS

First caution: This is a book about the management of health care, broadly. It is not about health care in the United States, or Canada (where I come from), or, for that matter, Malta, although all are mentioned. If you are an American interested in Obamacare or whatever, there are other books to read. But before you close this one, let me suggest that we all need to understand what is going on across all of health care. **I can think of no field that is more global in its professional practices yet more parochial in its administrative ones than health care.**

The new professional practices circulate quickly, at least in the developed world, while sensible ideas in management often fail to cross even borders, at least where I live (although nonsensical ones do too easily). Canada and the United States are claimed to share the longest unguarded border in the world. Not when it comes to health care! So **this book is about fundamental aspects of health care management that should know no borders.**

Next caution: Books these days are supposed to look terribly up-to-date. In this one you will notice no shortage of references from years ago. Please celebrate them! They are no more out-of-date than is good wine. I have used them because they have likewise stood the test of time, being as insightful today as when they were first written (while too much written today will thankfully be forgotten soon).

Last caution. I use quite a few footnotes in this book, not to make it academic, but to enrich the discussion and support the conclusions. They contain interesting evidence and colorful stories for readers who wish to have more detail.

Donald Hebb, McGill University's renowned psychologist, wrote, "A good theory is one that holds together long enough to get you to a better theory." My hope is that the ideas presented in this book will hold together long enough to help us get to better ideas for managing the care of our health.

PART I: MYTHS

MYTHS ABOUND IN MANAGEMENT—for example, that senior managers sit on "top" (of what?); that they "formulate" strategies for everyone else to "implement" (no feedback? no learning at this top?); that people are "human resources" (I am a human being); and that "if you can't measure it, you can't manage it" (whoever measured management, let alone measurement?).

Myths abound, too, in what is called the system of health care, not least that it is a system that is about the care of health. Combine these two sets of myths and you get what we have: a nonsystem that is being managed out of control. Discussed here are these myths: #1 that we have a system of health care; #2 that this system is failing; #3 that it can be fixed with heroic leadership, #4 with more administrative engineering, #5 with more categorizing and commodifying to facilitate more calculating, #6 with increasing its level of competition, #7 by managing it more like a business. These I argue have mostly been the problems, not the solutions: fixes such as these have been breaking much of health care. Last comes Myth #8, that health care is rightly left to the private sector for the sake of efficiency and choice, or else Myth #9, that it is rightly controlled by the public sector for the sake of equality and economy. How about greater recognition of what I shall be calling the *plural sector* (civil society, or the nonprofit sector), for the sake of quality and engagement?

Myth #1

We have a system of health care.

I haven't noticed. **Mostly we have a collection of disease cures, or at least treatments, often the more acute the better.** Overall, "health care" favors cure over care, acute diseases over chronic ones, and the treatment of diseases in particular over the prevention of illnesses and the promotion of health in general. As for research, development of cure receives much more attention than the investigation of cause.

Calling something a system does not make it a system where it needs to deliver. A system is characterized by natural linkages across its component parts. As we shall discuss later, a cow is a system, since its organs function together naturally. You and I are systems like this, too, at least in how we function physiologically, if not socially. About how much of the field of health care can we say that? What happens when all we individual physiological systems get together in a social context? Even the various medical specialties often have difficulty working with each other, let alone with nursing, community care, and management. As for the inclination to treat diseases instead of preventing them, let alone promoting health, see the box on "Health Promotion over the Cliff." It is not quite an allegory.

Health Promotion over the Cliff
(from Robbins, 1996: 1–2)

Once upon a time, there was a large and rich country where people kept falling over a steep cliff. They'd fall to the bottom and be injured, sometimes quite seriously, and many of them died. The nation's medical establishment responded to the situation by positioning, at the base of the cliff, the most sophisticated and expensive ambulance fleet ever developed, which could immediately rush those who had fallen to modern hospitals that were equipped with the latest technological wizardry. No expense was too great, they said, when people's health was at stake.

Now it happened that it occurred to certain people that another possibility would be to erect a fence at the top of the cliff. When they voiced the idea, however, they found themselves ignored. The ambulance drivers were not particularly keen on the idea, nor were the people who manufactured the ambulances, nor those who made their living and enjoyed prestige in the hospital industry. The medical authorities explained patiently that the problem was far more complex than people realized, that while building a fence might seem like an interesting idea it was actually far from practical, and that health was too important to be left in the hands of people who were not experts. . . .

So no fences were built, and as time passed this nation found itself spending an ever-increasing amount of its financial resources on hospitals and high-tech medical equipment. . . . As the costs of treating people kept rising, growing numbers of people could not afford medical care.

The more people kept falling off the cliff, the more a sense of urgency and tension developed, and the more of the country's money was poured into the heroic search for a drug that could be given to those who had fallen, to cure their injuries. When some people . . . questioned whether a cure would ever be found, the research industry answered with a massive public relations campaign showing men in white coats holding the broken bodies of children who had fallen, pleading, "Don't quit on us now, we're almost there."

When a few families who had lost loved ones tried to erect warning signs at the top of the cliff, they were arrested for trespassing. When some of the more enlightened physicians began to say that the medical authorities should publicly warn people that falling off the cliff was dangerous, representatives from powerful industries denounced them as "health police." . . . Finally, after many compromises, the medical establishment [issued] warnings. Anyone, they said, who had already broken both arms and both legs in previous falls should exercise utmost caution when falling.[1]

The French word for a surgical operation is *intervention*. Using the word in English, that is significantly what happens in health care: intermittent and disjointed interventions, whether in primary, secondary, tertiary, or so-called alternative medicine, as well as in public and community health. **We need more systemic practices in health care, especially to reconcile the delivery of quantity, quality, and equality.**

---

[1] Abraham Fuks of the McGill Faculty of Medicine has pointed out how medicine has reconceived some of its practices as preventative: "In the case of non-infectious diseases, preventive medicine has been transformed into a search for disease at its preclinical stages. . . . This strategy is reminiscent of the early warning systems of anti-missile defenses" (2009: 5).

2

Myth #2
The system of health care
is failing.

If there is one area of agreement in this field, this may be it: these "systems" are failing, all over the world. Users and providers alike complain bitterly about their health care.

At a party in Montreal a few years ago, I got into a conversation with a young radiologist who went on and on about how bad health care was in Quebec. "You did your residency in the United States," I finally intervened. "How about that?" She threw her hands in the air: "Don't get me started on the American system!" Sometime later I was in Italy, with people in the field who were likewise putting down their health care. So how does Italy compare with other countries, I asked. Oh, they replied: in the last ranking by the World Health Organization (2000), Italy ranked second best in the world behind France. Is second best still bad?

SUFFERING FROM SUCCESS

Quite the opposite: I believe that second best and much else is actually rather good—as far as it goes. **In most places in the developed world, the treatment of disease is succeeding, often rather dramatically. The trouble is that it is doing so expensively, and we don't want to pay for it.** In other words, **where it focuses its attention, health care is suffering from success more than from failure.**

And where it focuses less attention—in preventing illness in the first place—there have still been remarkable improvements, for example, in vaccines and the promotion of better eating and more exercise. It is just that here the pace of improvement is slower, and the efforts and resources expended are less—and no match for the commercial interests that promote poor eating and sedentary living.

On some of the broadest measures of life expectancy, infant mortality and others, performance in most countries has been steadily improving. A World Health Report in 1999 reviewed "the dramatic decline in mortality in the 20th century." To take one of its examples, Chilean women in 1998 could expect to live to age 79 on average, which was not only 46 years longer than their predecessors of 1910, but also 25 years longer than women of 1910 whose countries had the 1998 Chilean income level. The report attributed a part of the reduction in mortality to "income growth and improved educational levels—and consequent improvements in food intake and sanitation" but concluded that access "to new knowledge, drugs, and vaccines appears to have been substantially more important" (1999: 2).

Don't get me wrong about this claim of health care succeeding rather than failing, as did the head of an ICU who attended our International Masters for Health Leadership program (imhl .org). When he heard me say this, he became angry: he had to live with the errors, the distortions, and the other failures of health care. I could not argue with him about any of this, only to reply that I use the word *success* to mean getting better, not being perfect. Health care has its problems, to be sure, but it has been making remarkable progress where it focuses.

How about being offered this choice: (1) Health care circa 1960: when you feel chest pains, your GP comes to your home, gets you straight into a hospital, where you get attention from many doctors and nurses, who eventually send you back home to rest and hope for the best. You have received state-of-the-art health care. Or (2) health care now: no doctor comes to your house—you may even have to get yourself to a hospital, there to wait in an overcrowded emergency room until you get to cardiac surgery, where a stent is inserted, so that you can be sent home the next day, in rather good shape. You have received rather ordinary 21st-century health care.

Medicine has been particularly brilliant at developing expensive new treatments. Who among us is prepared to forego one of these to save our life? So we live longer, although sometimes more expensively sicker.

But not always: Consider a 90-year-old man in Vancouver who demanded an expensive hip replacement so that he could keep running. He was intent on maintaining his lifestyle, at the expense of the taxpayers of British Columbia. Could they fault him?

Pharmaceutical companies have had their expensive successes, too, except that these have been far too expensive in those countries disinclined to control the exorbitant pricing by this industry. (Bear in mind that these companies depend on state-granted monopolies—namely, patents—to charge what they do. When in the recent past has any country ever granted monopoly rights on necessities of life, such as electrical power or fixed-line telephone services, without seriously controlling prices? Being allowed to charge "what the market will bear" [a term used in *Businessweek* by Carey and Barrett in 2001] is simply patent nonsense. [See my article by this title, Mintzberg, 2006b.])

MORE FOR LESS?

Of course, while the costs of treatments go up, so too must the budgets to cover them, whether they are paid by taxes, insurance premiums, or personal payments. If we want more, we have to pay more. But in this age of consumptive greed, we want to pay less—or at least not that much more.

For the most part in the field of health care, we are not buying services so much as the possibility of needing services (i.e., insurance). Why, then, should *I* pay for *you*, who is sick, while I am healthy and probably invincible at that? In other words, **while the ill act as a concerted force for spending more locally, the healthy act as a general lobby for spending less nationally. This is not a happy combination: it makes the field of health care sick.**

Reconciling Supply and Demand

Before considering the obvious consequences of this, let me mention two other myths related to this one. The first is that we cannot afford the escalating costs of our health care services. Of course we can: it's a question of choices, individual and collective—really individual *or* collective. When we spend on cars and computers, we get instant gratification. How is health insurance, public or private, to compete with that?[1] It offers no fun! In the case of the United States, while health care costs far exceed those anywhere else, the very rich pay low taxes, and some major corporations hardly any taxes, while many Americans have long suffered for want of basic services.

---

[1] Perhaps this explains a report on the National Health Service of England website that compared patient satisfaction with public satisfaction. "People who have used the NHS tend to be much more positive than the general public." They speak from experience, while the latter are more inclined to form their opinions from exposure to the media (Edwards, 2009).

Myth #2

The other related myth is that the demand for health services is insatiable: provide more and we shall consume more. I don't know about you, but going to the doctor is not my idea of a good time (although I do like to chat with my particular GP): the waiting room, the needles, the prostate examination—no, thank you. I don't even cherish being admitted to a hospital. "Medical procedures are not hotcakes. People aren't going to line up eagerly demanding heart transplants just because someone else is paying" (CHSRF, 2001, citing Robert Evans of the University of British Columbia).

For every hypochondriac, how many other people avoid health services like the plague (so to speak)? Even that 90-year-old in Vancouver was not being unreasonable. Put yourself in his running shoes: this was truly a question of *health care*. So **excessive demand for health care services is not the problem so much as reasonable demand for services that are in short supply, thanks to our collective reluctance to pay for them.** (An exception can be noted here for the proclivity to order too many tests, especially in the United States, where there is so much litigation.)

Of course, there is a supply side to this issue. Give some physician the time and the fees for some treatment, and he or she may find lots of illness in need of it. Or give some hospital more beds and it will fill them. Is this a bad thing? Only if the added services are unnecessary or, worse, lead to the diagnosis of conditions that are better left untreated.[2]

---

[2] In a striking article, Atul Gawande (2009a) investigated two poor regions of Texas with rather similar health outcomes that had dramatically different costs: for U.S. Medicare in 2006, $15,000 per enrollee versus $7500. The reason, in his view: "across-the-board overuse of medicine." Casual decisions about prescriptions and financial benefits to the prescribers may in fact have increased risks. "Many physicians are remarkably oblivious to the financial implications of their decisions," while for others, "this is a business, after all." Recent reports on prostate tests and mammograms have suggested that they may be encouraging dysfunctional surgeries. On the other hand, those

So what are the consequences of all this? Quite simple: **The field of health care is being squeezed on all sides, by governments and markets, demanders and suppliers. As a result, many users are justified in feeling that they are not getting the services they need—not fast enough, not good enough, or just plain not enough.**

Pervasive Rationing

Rationing is a taboo word in much of health care. In Canada, governments go to great lengths to avoid mentioning the *R* word, let alone facing decisions about it. Yet **rationing is an intrinsic part of health care, everywhere, all the time**—for example, when a night nurse has to decide which of two beeping monitors to attend to first, or a physician has to determine who is to get a kidney that has become available for transplant, or a government or HMO has to specify the age at which people can no longer get some expensive treatment. The only alternative to this rationalizing is that everyone gets everything to cover every possible contingency. That is hardly feasible, at least if you are not Michael Jackson—and look what happened to him.[3]

---

people who avoid health care services may just be increasing the costs, since problems caught late can be much more expensive to treat.

[3] Peter Goldberg (mentioned earlier as head of that ICU in a Montreal hospital), wrote in his final paper in our IMHL Program entitled *Rationing in the Public Health System in Canada: The Search for an Ethical Construct*:

In thinking about these issues—aided, I must admit by the luxury of time afforded me to do exactly that in the confines of the IMHL—I came to understand that I had become, wittingly or not, an agent of rationing of medical services. While it was clear to me that none of my training or professional experience had prepared me for such a role, it also became clear to me that the public, or certainly those who took the time to consider such issues, would recoil at the arbitrariness with which I had come to occupy such a pivotal role in the allocation of their health care services. Furthermore, and perhaps instructively, I noted that nobody within the public health care system ever mentioned rationing. Nobody ever uttered the "r" word. When spoken of, such

Sometimes medicine strikes back. A surgeon called the executive director of his hospital: "I have a heart. I have a patient. I have an operating room. I have no budget." What is any manager who has a heart to do? This is rationing reduced to a game of Ping-Pong. Hit the problem back to someone else. Is the "system" failing, or are *we* failing in how we make choices, or refuse to?

We turn now to what have been the main administrative interventions applied to deal with this ostensible failure of health care: heroic leadership; administrative engineering; categorizing, commodifying, and calculating; increasing competition; and running health care like a business. I shall argue that, in some significant ways, much of this has delivered conspicuous failures.

---

euphemisms as allocation of scarce health care resources would be used so as to spare one's sensibilities—although it was unclear whose sensibilities were to be spared. (2011: 3)

Myth #3

Health care institutions, not to mention the whole system, can be fixed with more heroic leadership.

Leadership is all the rage today, especially in business, but well beyond it, too, and the field of health care is hardly immune. Count the thousands of books about leadership on Amazon, and then try to find the few on followership. **Are we so obsessed with leadership because we get so little of it? Or, do we get so little of it because we are so obsessed with it?**

Of course leadership matters. **The problem is the elevation of leadership to heroic status, as if leaders on "top" are superior to "human resources" below.** Such leaders are supposed to drive others to participate, for example by "empowering" them. Go tell that to professionals in hospitals, even to bees in a hive. They know what they have to do and just get on with doing it—unless, of course, they have long been *dis*empowered by their leadership.

The queen bee knows better: what she does is facilitate the worker bees' ability to get on with it, by emitting a chemical substance that holds the whole hive together. In human organizations, we call this *culture*. We human beings could use more leadership like this, especially in professional fields such as health care, which needs leadership to facilitate *communityship*. (I'll get back to this idea later.) Problematic can be the *position* of heroic leadership as well as the *person* in that position.

THE POSITION OF HEROIC LEADERSHIP

Jean-Louis Denis has written that "a very individualistic and grandiose vision of organizational leadership ... appears ill-suited to the workings of complex organizations marked by a fragmented authority structure" (2002: 17).

Managers and Leaders?

Making matters worse is the currently widespread belief, thanks to Bennis (1989), Zaleznik (1977, 2004), and Kotter (1990), that leadership is somehow superior to management. Leaders do the big things; managers do the rest—in medical terms, the "scut work." Or to use the more formal terms, leaders do the right things while managers do things right.

This may sound right, until you try to do the right things without doing them right. In practice, leadership cannot be separated from management; managers who don't lead discourage the people around them, while leaders who don't manage are disconnected from what is going on, and so are incapable of true leadership. **True leadership is management practiced well** (Mintzberg, 2009a).[1] We don't need more remote control in our organizations.

---

[1] When we created our master's program for people from all aspects of the management of health care worldwide, we were warned not to use the word

These days managers live in mortal fear of being accused of micromanaging—meddling in the work of their reports. Sure. **But finding out what's going on is not micromanaging. A far greater problem today is *"macroleading"*: the disengagement of those in authority, who deem from on high without living the consequences.** They play their lofty games of strategic planning (an oxymoron that we shall discuss later) and pronounce performance targets for everyone else to meet, without rolling up their sleeves and engaging themselves.

This false separation between leading and managing has been undermining American corporations for years, with so many of them having become overled and undermanaged (Mintzberg, 2011, 2013). Worse still can be its effects on health care institutions, where the hierarchy of professional status flows up (e.g., in medicine, from interns to residents to junior and more senior staff), while the hierarchy of administrative authority flows down, from executive director to department head to first-line manager, passing each other like ships in the night, instead of stopping to cooperate for the sake of better health care.

Formulators and Implementers?

It is important to appreciate that **two sides are at fault here: professionals who lord their status over the managers and managers who lord their authority over the professionals.** Following business practice, the managers are supposed to "formulate" the strategies while the professionals are supposed to "implement" them.[2] And when this fails, as it so often does,

---

management, because of its negative connotation in health care. So we called it the International Masters for Health Leadership, the word *for* being used to suggest that the program seeks to be a leading forum for the discussion of major issues in the field.

[2]Nembhard et al. (2009) asked, "Why does the quality of health care continue to lag?" They answered by noting that in other "industries," the managers are

implementation is inevitably blamed. After all, who's doing the blaming? The formulators.

Yet every failure of implementation is also a failure of formulation. After all, shouldn't the formulators have taken into account the capabilities of the implementers, whom they were supposed to know? In health care, however, as we shall discuss at greater length later, it is the implementers who do much of the formulating: strategies emanate largely from the supposed bottom, in the form of strategic initiatives (for example, day surgeries) championed by operating professionals. Thus, in discussing health care in the U.S. Veterans Administration, Longman (2012: 12) noted that when faced with dwindling resources to deal with aging patients, there arose "an explosion of organizational and technological innovation, most of it started by individual doctors acting on their own."

Aside from that, operating professionals often blame the managers for whatever goes wrong, Instead, they themselves should be blamed for remaining aloof from the significant needs of their organizations. Please therefore, **blame the blaming, so that it can be replaced with collaborating.** As long as the administrators see themselves as above the professionals, while the professionals see themselves as superior to the administrators, health care institutions will not be able to deal with their problems systemically. **Health care does not need superior leaders, domineering managers, or haughty professionals. Enough of "us" and "them." It needs all of its people to understand, respect, and cooperate with each other.**

---

in charge, "workers are compelled to comply with [the managers'] implementation efforts. Health care managers do not have such compelling authority" (p. 29), so that efforts to implement their innovations frequently get blocked. Good thing, judging by our discussions to come in Myths #4, #5, and #7.

THE PERSON AS HEROIC LEADER

If heroic leadership in general does not do it, then surely the right person in the job can. So welcome to the world of the heroic leader.

Nembhard et al. (2009) wrote the following about health care in a journal of the largest association of management academics: "transformational leaders . . . by being charismatic . . . motivate the workforce . . . and elicit positive feelings," thus cultivating "a climate in which the workforce feels comfortable offering feedback to leaders about how to improve innovation implementation" (p. 35). Read this to a physician in this "workforce," if you can find one who feels uncomfortable about telling his or her leader a thing or two. Of course good leaders can be inspirational—but not if they believe this kind of nonsense.

THE QUEST FOR A REGULAR LEADER

Find a great organization and you will soon find a journalist attributing its success to a great leader. That is easier than trying to find out what really happened. Perhaps conditions improved and so the leader got lucky. Or maybe some internal team grabbed hold of the problems and improved the place. A good leader can certainly encourage such teamwork, but this does not make success a solitary exercise, nor does it make a team builder a genius.

The worst consequence of our "romance of leadership" (as Meindl et al., 1985, put it) is that it encourages leaders, even good ones, to take themselves too seriously. They risk becoming narcissistic failures. Organizations are complex entities. Many of the great ones did have founders who played key roles in establishing their greatness. But this does not render their successors charismatic wonders.

Let me take my own shot at the $64 billion question that fascinates the readers of those thousands of books on Amazon: What is it that makes for effective leadership? (The following comes from my book *Simply Managing*, 2013.) **Many successful leaders are not "transformational" or "charismatic" so much as healthy and engaged: they connect with and respect people, whom they see as colleagues, not "subordinates," let alone a "workforce."** And so they cooperate naturally with them. I believe that **the great organizations are robust *communities* of human *beings*, not generic collections of "human resources."** It is the collective efforts of these human beings that make its leadership appear to be great.

So **let's take leadership off its heroic pedestal, combine it with management, and bring both together into the rest of the organization, where they belong.** That way we can end the quest for superpeople to fill "superior" positions at the "top."

Myth #4

The health care system can be fixed with more administrative engineering.

In this myth, the fix remains in the hierarchy of authority, but not with leaders or managers so much as with the administrative "experts" whom they empower to do their bidding. (Much of this bidding will be described here, except for that relating to categorization, commodification, and calculation, which will be discussed in the myth that follows.)

The "system" is broken, so bring on the administrative experts to fix it: analysts, planners, economists, reengineers, technocrats, accountants, MBAs, and management consultants, preferably, it sometimes seems, with no experience on the ground.[1] Let's

---

[1] Simon Head (2003) listed the credentials and background experiences of the authors of a book entitled *Changing Health Care*, brought out by Andersen Consulting (now Accentura) in 1997: mergers and acquisitions, leadership development ,and organization design. One's work focused on "creating strategies to reduce medical costs"; another authored *Zap! Empowerment in Health Care*. None had any medical qualifications. "Knowledge of medicine is no

call them all administrative engineers, because they practice a form of social engineering for the administration of health care. What too many of them do is: Measure like mad. Reorganize constantly. Drive change from the "top," for the sake of "empowerment" at the bottom. Promote the management technique of the month while "reinventing" health care every year or two. All this while the real experts, who deliver the services on that ground, struggle to cope with the pressures, not least from the disruptions caused by these very "solutions."

To frame the discussion that follows, let me suggest something quite different, in fact something historically tried and true: **Much of the significant change in health care has to come initially from the ground up, not the top down, let alone from experts who have not practiced health care.** Consider those day surgeries, one of the major developments of recent times that has improved quality as well as cutting costs. This was championed by clinicians, initially concerned about the consequences of prolonged bed rest (see www.daysurgeryuk.org).

Administrative engineers certainly have important roles to play in health care, especially to help keep the lid on costs, to challenge exploitation by professionals and suppliers, and to spread knowledge about significant changes coming from the ground—so long as they respect and support the people who work on that ground.

FADS, FALLACIES, AND FOOLISHNESS

This is the title of a book by Ted Marmor of Yale University, whose "fundamental contention" was "that the discussion of modern medicine's most prominent topics—cost, quality, access, and organization—is marked by linguistic muddle and conceptual

---

more required of the health care consultant than knowledge of meatpacking is required of those having to sort out Burger King" (2003: 123).

confusion." Marmor distinguished two types of "business talk": management jargon that comes out of the business schools and consulting firms, and marketing jargon, or hype, that is now also pervasive (2007: 2).[2]

There is no shortage of managerial fads in health care: "managed care," "patient-centered care," "purchasers and providers," and so on. Such "slogans," labeled to "imply success by their very use" (anyone for "unmanaged" care?), are "meant to convince rather than to describe or explain" (p. 10).

Marmor singles out this managed care for special attention. He traces early use of the term to the *New York Times* in 1985; in 1998 the label appeared in that newspaper 587 times (p. 11). "What exactly managed care is, however, has never been entirely clear, even among its strongest proponents." For example, to some it is per capita payments, yet "many, if not most, American health insurance plans that are labeled 'managed care' in fact do not rely on capitation" (p. 12).

Lancet, in its October 29, 1994 issue, described managed care in the U.K. as "the hot new export from the United States, promoted by major consultants as the most efficient way to integrate primary care, sub-specialization, and everything in between" (p. 13). Six years later, *Business Week* (2000) polled American public attitudes to Managed Care Organizations

---

[2] Even where it should not be. A book by Harvard's Michael Porter with Elizabeth Teisberg (2006) described their proposed reform, "value-based competition," as "the only antidote to inefficiency and quality problems" of health care. "Errors will fall dramatically"; "professional pride will motivate improvement.... innovation will occur even faster" [p. 8] ... "Quality will improve across the board ... society will have more resources ... universal insurance coverage" will become "more affordable." "Primary and preventative care can be extended to all Americans ... " (p. 9). This is an "imperative" (p. 235), that will provide "stunning improvements" (p. 382). All of this for ideas that are sometimes interesting and often questionable (as we shall discuss later), none of them tested on the scale proposed. (See also the abstract in their 2007 article in the *Journal of the American Medical Association*.)

(MCO): 71 percent judged their service to be "poor" or "fair," only 18 percent "good" or "excellent." This level of popularity matched that of the tobacco companies (in Head, 2003: 199).

Marmor concluded that "an unfortunate consequence of the injection of managerial fads into medical care is the suggestion that there is some right way, some panacea, for rationalizing the delivery of decent, affordable medical care." But because "the objectives of any institution are multiple, shifting, and often contradictory," good management depends on how well the manager's particular approach balances these particular needs (pp. 19, 22, 20).

Thanks to all these fads and fallacies, we have too many "solutions" in health care whose simplicity does not match the complexity of the work in question. The consequence is that many fail, or worse, succeed in implementation, only to drag that work down. Common examples, discussed below, have come from re-engineering, reorganizations, mergers, and the creation of pretend markets. (Performance measurements will be discussed in a later section.)

RE-ENGINEERING THE HEALTH CARE FACTORY

Simon Head is particularly harsh in his criticism of re-engineering applied to health care, citing some of its worst practices: "Medical reengineers simplify existing processes and speed them up. Patients get to spend fewer days in the hospital ... [they] are allowed fewer visits to the doctor ... and those with routine symptoms find themselves diagnosed over the telephone" (2003: 124). Head sees the ultimate intention of this as marginalizing the role of doctors and their interface with the patient.[3] To appreciate

---

[3] In an article about "the political uses of management consulting," Kantola and Seeck (2011) refer to such approaches as "Taylorism ... the simplification of labor and resource into isolated problems of mechanical efficiencies." These "technocratic fix[es], a single optimum solution 'best practice' ... for political

the spirit of this, have a look at the accompanying box called "Re-engineering an Orchestra."

Re-engineering an Orchestra

A young, enthusiastic MBA was finally given the opportunity to apply his learning. He was asked to carry out a survey of a group with which he was not normally familiar and submit recommendations as to how its efficiency could be increased. He selected as his target a symphony orchestra. Having read up on the tools of the trade, he attended his first concert and submitted the following analysis:

a. For considerable periods, the four oboe players had nothing to do. The number of oboes should therefore be reduced, and the work spread more evenly over the whole concert program, thus eliminating the peaks and valleys of activity.

b. All twenty violins were playing identical notes. This would seem to be an unnecessary duplication, so the staff of this section should be cut drastically.

c. Obsolescence of equipment is another matter warranting further investigation. The program noted that the leading violinist's instrument was several hundred years old. Now, if normal depreciation schedules had been applied, the value of this instrument would have been reduced to zero and the purchase of more modern equipment recommended long ago.

d. Much effort was absorbed in the playing of demisemiquavers, which seems to be an unnecessary refinement. It is recommended that all notes be rounded up to the nearest semiquaver. If this were done, it would be possible to use trainees and lower-grade operatives more extensively. . . .

---

problems . . . have been endorsed by liberal, socialist, authoritarian, and even communist and fascist states" (p. 31).

e. Finally, there seemed to be too much repetition of some of the musical passages. Therefore, scores should be pruned to a considerable extent. No useful purpose is served by repeating on the horns something which has already been handled by the strings. It is estimated that, if all redundant passages were eliminated, the whole concert time of two hours could be reduced to twenty minutes and there would be no need for an intermission.

Published more or less as above in the mid-1950s in an American professors' bulletin, a Canadian military journal, and *Harper's Magazine*, based on an anonymous memorandum circulating in London and probably published originally in *Her Majesty's Treasury of the Courts*.

WHEN IN DOUBT, REORGANIZE

Reorganization is a particularly popular form of administrative engineering, in health care no less than in business. When in doubt, reorganize: shuffle people and positions around on pieces of paper. **Is this so popular because it's so easy, at least for the administrative engineers and their managers? And does it make much difference, particularly in a field where managerial authority can often be easily trumped by medical influence?**

Actually, the answer to the second question is yes: it can drive health care professionals to distraction. Like trying to read in bed on a Sunday morning while the kids are running around, trying to get your operating work done while the place is repeatedly being reorganized can be awfully disruptive.

In one sense, reorganization is always a solution. That is because **every basis for organizing is flawed—a compromise.** In business, if you are a food company organized in Asia by product lines (cheese and chocolate), then you are probably not giving enough attention to regions. After all, the Indians eat lots of cheese but not much chocolate, while the Chinese eat little of both. So you reorganize by region . . . and then products become the problem. Why is the headquarters in Mumbai pushing cheese in China? Later someone will get the bright idea to reorganize back. In other words, **reorganization is the perfect disjointed intervention for a "system" built on disjointed interventions:** trading off the devil you know for the one you don't, or at least have forgotten.[4]

The fallacy here lies in the assumption that structure is organization: that drawing boxes on paper, about who reports to whom, magically gets people coordinating with each other. Change a few names, a few titles, and off you go. Sure—too often down some black hole. Figure 1a shows an organization. Study it carefully. Then look at Figure 1b. It shows a *reorganization*.

These charts show top, middle, and bottom management. I imagine that you say "top management" in your organization, and "middle management" too. Therefore, you must say "bottom

FIGURE 1a **An Organization**

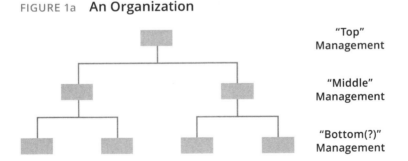

"Top" Management

"Middle" Management

"Bottom(?)" Management

---

[4] Unless you want it all, for example with a "matrix stature." One hospital in Toronto developed a double matrix—a cube structure—comprising "programs" (aging, trauma, etc.), "clinical units" (surgery, oncology, etc.), and "traditional" units (nursing, pharmacy, etc.). This became quite famous. When sometime later I met the executive director who created this, I asked: "So how's your famous cube structure?" "Oh," he answered, "we got rid of that long ago."

FIGURE 1b **A Reorganization?**

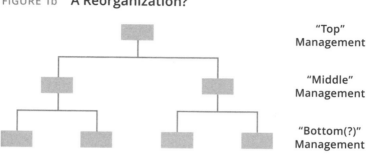

"Top"
Management

"Middle"
Management

"Bottom(?)"
Management

management" as well. You don't? How can that be? Every top and middle has to have a bottom, and, believe me, those who manage at the bottom are well aware of that, no matter what they are called. So my suggestion to you is this: **get honest and call it bottom management, or else get sensible and rid your place of the term** *top management.*

When we say top management, we see these people up there somewhere, on a ceiling, or above it, removed from what's going on. That, unfortunately, is where many see themselves too. Is this any way to manage an organization? Remember, "top" is a metaphor, usually found only on the charts (not to mention the pay scales). In hospitals, these top managers don't usually even sit on the top floor, but rather near the main door (perhaps to be able to make a quick getaway).

In the National Health Service of England (NHS), which employs more than a million people, the reorganizations have become legion—to the point where an editorial in the *British Medical Journal* once described the NHS as being in a state of constant *dis*organization (Smith et al., 2001).

When I first visited the NHS in the early 1990s, the headquarters in London sat on top of 14 "Regions" which sat on top of 175 "Districts" which sat on top of the institutions that delivered the services. The 50 "Areas" between Regions and Districts had just been eliminated, thanks to a consulting study. In a 2006 visit to the NHS, many reorganizations later, I found only "Strategic Health Authorities," 28 in number—in other words, no more Regions or Districts, just something akin to Areas by another name (which were soon reorganized into 17 and then into 10). As Marmor saw it, "The NHS appears to have been on a centralizing mission for decades now, masking that for a time with one or another reorganization" (2007: 16).[5] But the NHS has been put to shame by a couple of reorganizations in Quebec where I live, as described in the accompanying box.

The Worst Reorganization Ever?

A few years ago, concerned about the need for better coordination of services in the health care regions of Quebec—across hospitals, community care clinics, long-term facilities, and other institutions—the government merged them into CSSSs (Centres de santé et de services sociaux), each with a single "directeur

---

[5] "In 2002, the government of British Columbia amalgamated the province's 52 regional health boards into five large health authorities. The smallest serves over 300,000 people living in the north of the province, the largest over 1.5 million people in its Lower Mainland. These authorities have used their power to contract out some services, cut many others, and generally serve as the government's major instrument in the reduction of provincial health costs." In B.C., "'Efficiency' means 'centralization.'" Yet "the larger, more centralized the health system, the less likely it is to be responsive to local needs" (Smecher, 2007: 7). On the other hand, the following appeared in the same publication, called "Canada's community economic development magazine": "Regional Health Authorities frequently take the role of the 'bad guys' in matters of community control. They are the ones who close local hospitals and appropriate local assets. Yet, they are still the 'least centralized' of government health bureaucracies and their office-holders (our neighbors) the most subject to public pressure. They are a feature on the health care landscape that local innovators will drive their initiatives around, over, beneath, or—with good management—through" (Zitner and Kelderman, 2007: 5). See also http://www.health.org.uk/blog/glazier-or-window-breaker

général" and budget. Needless to say, the director generals of the original institutions were worried about losing their jobs.

I addressed them at a conference, and suggested there was no reason to worry: the net result in a CSSS with four institutions would be, not one director general, but five. For how was one person to manage four physically separate facilities that offered different services? Each would need its own manager, whether or not called a director general. (Or so I thought then, underestimating how wacky politicians can be—as we shall soon see.)

The CSSS concept seemed fine in mid-air, where hierarchy reigns supreme. But how about on the ground? Was some new director general to issue orders from some lofty office so that a patient in a hospital would be transferred seamlessly to a long-term care facility? Or were the nurses on the two ends of this transfer to cooperate diligently because way above them, on some chart in some drawer, was a leader who was their boss's boss's boss?

Grenier and Wong (2010) of the McGill Social Work Department studied these CSSS reforms. They described them as "steeped in technocratic and rational processes of managerialism that create discrepancies between stated intentions and lived experiences" (2010: 2).

The "structural changes took place at the higher levels of administration in a rapid and formal fashion" that largely excluded those people most affected. This speed was "intended to stifle dissent" (p. 16). Managers expressed concerns about "losing sight of the day-to-day work," being "bogged down with much more administrative duties," and complained about a "new structure which does complicate things" (pp. 14, 13).

In fact, the lack of "a clear understanding of [the units'] overlapping responsibilities . . . *discouraged* inter-agency collaboration" (p. 20, italics added).[6] For the senior people, however, "the

---

[6] Grenier and Wong noted that as those CSSS "reforms progressed, the difficulties of implementing change into existing . . . structures became evident"

reform [was] perceived as a success—structural changes were achieved as intended" (p. 24).

Those were the good old days. At least someone, even if not called director general, could still manage the individual institutions. No longer. The premier of a new Quebec government, a physician, together with his minister of health, another physician, went a step further and wiped out the management of almost all the Quebec health care institutions, combing these into regional agglomerations, each with its own president-directeur général.

Yesterday you were managing a hospital. Today, if you are one of the lucky ones who didn't get fired, you find yourself managing that hospital plus a smaller specialized one plus a long-term care facility plus institutions for community, rehabilitation, palliation, and geriatrics—in one case, nine different ones spread around some geographic area. Bang: with the stroke of a pen, 200 DGs and PDG magically became 28. (And 200 boards of directors magically become 28, with most of these people now named by the minister. More on this later.) They called these new agglomerations "Centres intégrés de santé et de services sociaux" (CISSS). In other words, our leaders added an I for *integration*! Someone who has been living these changes wrote to me about the consequences:

> "I have been through many reorganization efforts and transformations since I have been a 'medical administrator', but none came even close to being so destructive and dehumanizing . . . What is amazing is that we are all paralyzed. A few of us have spoken up, but our words have no impact. The silence and passivity are frightening."

Grenier and Wong's study, cited above, about the consequences of the previous reform that went half as far—*evidence!*—was ignored. Indeed this new reform was put into effect across

---

(p. 15). The reforms proceeded in a "top down process," while "professional insights on service gaps and knowledge of best practices remained unsolicited" (pp. 15, 16)

all of Quebec without any testing. Can you imagine these two physicians doing something like this in their medical practices? They claimed to have saved us tons of money, not to mention doing all this for the sake of citizens, service, and reduced bureaucracy. Well, health care may be expensive, but words are cheap.

So I proposed a terrific idea for our premier. Why do you need all these ministers—of education, justice, finance, mining, etc., especially health. Centralize them all in your own office, and save us tons more money. Take a dose of your own medicine.

(Written up in Mintzberg, 2016a and 2016b)

USE PRETEND MARKETS WHEN YOU CAN'T GET AWAY WITH REAL ONES

Near the time of that first visit to the NHS, I spent a day observing the head of one of those districts (fully described in www .mintzberg-managing.com, pp. 78–80). A long meeting took place with an official from the headquarters in London, who came because the district was considered to be advanced in implementing a new initiative from the NHS. The official came to capture the district's learning. For the district general manager, this meeting provided an opportunity to impress the people who provided the money.

In this fancy piece of administrative engineering, the districts were to become "purchasers," while the hospitals and other units, which formerly reported to these districts, were to become "providers," so that they could negotiate with each other for the provision of services. The Conservative government of the day could not turn the NHS into a real market (see Myth #6 on competition and Myth #7 on being a business), so it had created these pretend markets instead. In fact, the district people at this meeting didn't seem quite sure what they were doing, but the ministry official appeared to be a lot less sure, so they all played the game.

They discussed "quality" in terms of "ten key indicators," which apparently came from another consulting study. At one point, a district staff member said "I don't think that any of us has talked to 'consumers' properly," to which another replied, "I did . . . about two years ago." (Presumably this person did not talk to her friends or relatives, not even to herself. Who in England doesn't use the NHS?) Then they spent "two minutes on risk," with one district staffer saying, "I don't understand it," and the official from the ministry commenting, "I have a view of it: we need to build some kind of decision analysis process that takes into account political risks."

Let me assure you that I did not lift this from Dilbert. I wrote down these words carefully, as I heard them.[7] This is the Alice in Wonderland of Health Care Management, or as one group of management researchers suggested more formally, the NHS learned how to manage change but forgot how to manage health care (Pettigrew et al., 1988).

Carolyn Tuohy has concluded that the intervention of these "purchasers"—who are "third-party payers," not the actual users of the services—complicates matters by splitting their interest in getting value-for-money away from the patients' interest in getting quality care. In fact, she claimed that the whole purchase-provider concept, while not really introducing much new competition, "can be seen as a quest . . . to control professional power" (2007; see also Pollock, 2004).

---

[7] England is hardly alone in such talk. A Canadian health care manager in the Arctic described to me a meeting he had with senior health ministry officials from provinces across the country: "The ideas they discuss are so esoteric that they are not useful. You go home and wonder what to do about all this. I'm into nuts and bolts, and they are talking abstractions."

MERGE LIKE MAD

Popular, too, are mergers, as they have been in business, often with a similar rate of failure. Too often, mergers in both seem to proceed on the assumption that if one organization is not working well, merge it with another that is not working well: together they will work marvelously. Or if one is small, bury it inside another that is large, because bigger is inevitably better (for the power of the "CEO," at least). Merging is also easy, for starters: a few signatures and two physically separate institutions magically become one. On paper. The chaos that can follow is another matter (as we saw in those CISSS agglomerations).

Mergers often add an additional layer to the administrative hierarchy, so that the administrators who previously managed independent institutions must now report to a new administrator who is supposed to be managing them. The former thus have to spend more time looking up, with less time for their own operations. And the latter, further removed from the operations, are even more inclined to manage by the numbers instead of the facts.

To merge institutions for the sake of gaining real complementarities makes good sense. But how often are these realized in such mergers? Porter and Teisberg, despite being sympathetic to the business perspective in health care, concluded that "with few exceptions, hospital mergers have resulted in little or no true consolidation and integration at the service line level."[8] In fact, many mergers have amounted to power grabs of one kind

---

[8] See also Herzlinger (2007: 66), an even greater fan of health care as a business, who cites evidence that these mergers have led to price increases, while the CHSRF report (2002) describes mergers as increasing administrative costs and impacting negatively on staff morale and turnover as well as patient outcomes. In a Canadian report, "Between 1990 and 1999—the peak of 'merger madness'—the number of . . . hospitals declined from 1231 to 929," resulting in increasing administrative costs and impacting negatively on staff morale and turnover as well as patient outcomes. This publication also noted that in the

or another by the larger institution, to "boost bargaining power vis-à-vis health plans" (2006: 39), not to mention enhancing the status of those who end up running the larger institutions.

In private health care, how many hospitals have been combined into large chains, supposedly to achieve economies of scale? That they often have—*economies*, quite literally, by saving quantities at the expense of qualities. All things considered, **"the urge to merge is an astounding run-away phenomenon given the weak research base to support it"** (CHSRF, 2002).

THE MYTH OF SCALE

Mainstream economists, many administrators, large corporations, and many governments love scale. Bigger inevitably looks better: bigger budgets, more beds, grander institutions, vaster regions, and, of course, higher salaries for those who come out on "top." The favored term is *economies of* scale, not effectiveness of scale. Again, it's the costs that count, not the qualities (which are tougher to measure, as will be discussed later).

When I checked the NHS website in January 2013, it boasted about employing 1.2 million people, including 150,000 hospital doctors, 315,000 nurses, and 18,800 ambulance staff. "The number of patients using the NHS is equally mind-boggling," it gushed: over a million every 36 hours, or 463 a minute, including 3000 heart operations and 700,000 dental visits a week. "Only the Chinese People's Liberation Army, the Walmart supermarket chain, and the Indian Railways directly employ more people." Some standards!

Regina Herzlinger of the Harvard Business School has complained that "Health care is still an astonishingly fragmented industry. More than half of U.S. physicians work in practices

---

U.K., "some 99 trust mergers have taken place since 1997, 14 in London alone," with questionable results in large facilities and on staff morale (CHSRF, 2002).

of three or fewer doctors; a quarter of the nation's 5,000 community hospitals and nearly half of its 17,000 nursing homes are independent" (2006: 59). As if all of this is a terrible thing! Herzlinger claimed, "You can roll a number of independent players up into a single organization ... to generate economies of scale" (p. 59). Picture that!

No one has rolled up my GP. He works conscientiously in a clinic with two other physicians. I doubt that I am alone in preferring independent institutions to large chains. They are usually more human, like your neighborhood restaurant compared with some fast-food corporation.

Interviews with five "CEOs" of not-for-profit American hospitals found them to be in agreement "that to compete successfully, their organizations needed to grow ... in revenues as well as market share." They offered several reasons for this: the need for increased service volumes to reduce costs; the ability to maintain "bond ratings," which required a minimum of 2–3 percent return-on-investment (i.e., profit); and the requirement to buy the "latest technology ... a key to competing successfully" (Best, 2007: 9). There are sometimes good reasons to favor scale in health care, but are these the ones?

Sure, many medical procedures need to be performed frequently so that the physicians can hone their skills. And some expensive technologies certainly require scale, hopefully to better serve the patients, rather than help the institutions compete.[9]

---

[9] The [Veterans Administration] scale has ... been an important precondition for the deployment of its highly effective health IT platform (VistA), the cost of which it has been able to spread across a large base of hospitals and clinics. Similarly, the outcomes databases generated by VistA have far greater scientific value because they are drawn from a very broad population. The substantial advantage of market power that the VA enjoys in negotiation with drug companies and other medical suppliers is also a function of scale (Longman, 2012: 138).

But there are also reasons why scale is no holy grail in health care. **Too frequently economies of scale have been allowed to trump human scale because of the sheer power or convenience of being big.** For example, how often have government authorities, feeling the need to reduce the number of public hospital beds, closed several small hospitals instead of a single big one. After all, the supporters of the large institution can make a greater fuss in the media.[10]

Economies of scale may apply to the mass production of automobiles, but I am not an automobile, thank you. I respond to how I am treated. "The object travelling down the medical assembly line is not a chassis or an engine, it is ourselves" (Head, 2003: 125). Especially when we are sick, but even when we are well, we often find large institutions to be impersonal and alienating. That can influence the effectiveness of the treatments we receive. No wonder there has been a movement away from large hospitals, just as from large schools. **To achieve real quality in health care, we require personalized services on a human scale, not impersonal interventions on an economic scale.**

Moreover, large scale can impose a certain conformity on activities. This may make them easier to administer, but it can also stifle the need for local adaptation. Some physician abused a patient so all such physicians have to keep their doors open. (As in airports: every time a terrorist gets a new idea, millions of passengers have to endure some new humiliation.) Small institutions can often deal with certain problems in less formal, more effective ways. **For most everything in health care (and out), the imperative that scale, or measurement, or leadership, etc., is some sort of "one best way" is simplistic and dysfunctional.**

---

[10] They generally have better political contacts too and greater political savvy. See Granovetter (1973) on "The Strength of Weak Ties," about how people in tighter communities can lack the connections to broader social institutions that people in looser communities have.

Let's take a look at scale in the two places where it is most favored: in institutions and geographic regions.

Institutional Scale

In health care institutions, especially hospitals, scale gets considerable attention from those administrative engineers who deal with problems by trying to make them bigger—the institutions, I mean, although often the problems, too.

We have already discussed what can be called the *politics* of scale: the inclination to merge small hospitals into larger ones for the power of the administrators. This can also amount to the *convenience* of scale: it takes time and effort for central administrators to deal with numerous small institutions—hours and hours of their time. How much more convenient to roll them all up and deal with just one, even if that can make many service providers miserable for years.

Large scale also encourages the very kind of administrative interventions that I criticized earlier. As institutions grow larger, they layer one level of administrator upon another in their formal hierarchies.[11] Each, being further removed from the operations, turns increasingly to reorganizing, reengineering, measuring, and other easy fixes.

---

[11] Partly driving this is the traditional belief in so-called "spans of control": that some limited number of people should report to each manager. (Seven has been the popular number.) There are two problems with this. First, there is more to management than control; and second, some people hardly need to be controlled by their managers. Thus, in our faculty at McGill, we have about 60 professors reporting to one dean, with no intermediate level of management. That dean is expected to spend a good deal of time raising funds more than controlling the professors (see Mintzberg, 1983: 65–72). Of course, "delayering" has become fashionable—getting rid of the layers of management. The trouble is that it is often used when narrow spans are necessary, as in project teams, with the result that the managers left behind get overburdened.

I am not arguing here that small is always beautiful, only pleading that bigger is not necessarily better. I recognize that scale may be needed to make use of expensive equipment, to attract certain talent, also to fund research that could be expensive for small institutions. But these advantages have to be weighed against human factors.[12]

The scale problem seems to apply to pharmaceutical research too. A number of the largest companies have for years been facing difficulties in their research. A chief executive of Merck, the firm hitherto most renowned for its research, commented that "scale has been no indicator of the ability to discover breakthrough drugs. In fact, it has been the other way—you get bogged down" (in Clifford, 2000). Much of the interesting pharmaceutical research now comes out of smaller firms.

Geographic Scale

The National Health Service of England serves 55 million people. (Scotland, Wales, and Northern Ireland serve their own smaller populations separately.) Medicare in the Canadian province of Alberta serves 4 million; in Ontario, 14 million; in Prince Edward Island (PEI), also a province, 146,000. In fact, PEI does this for less cost per capita than most of the other provinces. Life may be easier in the birthplace of Anne of Green Gables than in downtown Calgary or Toronto, but these figures are hardly a testimonial to the glories of large scale. And, by the way, in the last WHO national rankings of health care (2000),

---

[12] I learned how large institutions can sometimes be less efficient when a senior administrator at our university threatened to merge our little management library into the big central one. We went about collecting data to prove him wrong. On all measures, our little library did better. Its people did naturally what big organizations tie themselves in knots trying to get their people to do—sharing jobs, helping each other out, having the manager pitch in when short-staffed.

the five best-performing countries in the world were France and Italy—midsized countries—followed by San Marino, Andorra, and Malta, all tiny ones.

How come PEI gets to run its own health care service, while London, with 60 times the population, does not? For no other reason than because Canada is a federation and PEI is one of the provinces, with the constitutional power to manage its health care, just like Alberta and Ontario, while London is a city in England without that power.

This constitutional power in Canada is subject to five national principles in the Canada Health Act of 1985: that the health service be public, comprehensive, universal (across the population), portable (from one province to another), and accessible (without charge). These principles have been enforced by the federal government (still so, but less than before), which provides some of the funding. I have been told that about 20 people administer this in Ottawa, the federal capital, leaving the rest of the administration to the provinces.

If PEI is able to run its health care for 146,000 people, how come Ontario does so for 14 million, let alone England for 55 million? In fact, the Canadian provinces have recognized the problem and came up with a solution, much like that of the NHS. They have organized their health services into smaller geographic regions. In so doing, they have had a perfect model to follow, from Ottawa: keep 20 people plus those five basic principals in the provincial capitals, and let the regions in the provinces do the rest. (Better still, consider Switzerland, a small country that actually leaves responsibility for health care to its cantons, five of which have populations below 50,000, one just 15,000.)

Good luck. The real model, de facto, has been the NHS, not Ottawa: the provinces keep large numbers of administrators in their capitals, piled atop many more in the regions, all busy reorganizing and measuring, etc.[13] This has certainly helped to keep the lid on health care costs (other than the administrative ones), while driving an awful lot of the operating people to distraction, at what cost to the quality of service we hardly know—that's a lot harder to measure.[14]

KEEPING THE BABY

So what can we conclude about administrative engineering? Not that it is wrong or unnecessary. As noted earlier, the administrative engineers have to help keep the lid on costs, to challenge exploitative behaviors, and to help spread innovations

---

[13] Sheila Damon reports in 2016 a drive toward devolution and local collaboration in the NHS, with massive cuts in the Department of Health.

[14] Jean-Louis Denis (2002) assessed the various results of regionalization in the Canadian provinces, and concluded that it has "not yet proved itself in terms of co-ordination and integration of health care and services"; "not brought about the greater democratization of administrative structures and service systems expected"; "has had imperfect results in producing change." The board members of the regional authorities "feel they are better informed about costs and service utilization than about service benefits, citizens' preferences and the opinions of the players in the community," which suggests that they are "more likely to respond to the wishes of the central government than to local preferences" (p. 5). "Most respondents believe that they are held accountable for elements that are not entirely within their control, and that the [provincial] government's rules are too constraining" (p. 6). In personal correspondence responding to the above text, Sholom Glouberman has pointed out:

When the NHS was relatively stable and working reasonably well, one of the advantages of scale was that an employee of the NHS could move throughout the system and be assured of permanent employment... People saw themselves as employees of the system and belonging to it. There was a strong sense of altruism and of contributing to the society. People wore little badges saying that they loved the NHS. This was true up until the late 1990s. In this case the [regionalization] caused as much harm as the increased industrialization of the system.

Fair enough, but that identification can be had on a smaller scale too (little badges saying people love PEI health care).

beyond their place of origin. But they are not helpful when they assume they know better than the people on the ground, and feel compelled to control them. **We don't need the bathwater of administrative engineering, but we do need the baby. Some control is necessary, especially when operating professionals are irresponsible and resist necessary changes.** But as a colleague likes to say: "You can never beat the doctors!" So **the administrative engineers do better by finding responsible professionals and figuring out how to collaborate with them.**

Myth #5

The health care system can be fixed with more categorizing and commodifying to facilitate more calculating.

Michael Porter, economist and professor at the Harvard Business School, together with colleagues, has published prominently on health care in recent years (e.g., Kaplan and Porter, 2011; Porter, 2010; Porter and Teisberg, 2004, 2006;). Under the banner of promoting greater competition in the field (which we shall discuss in the next section), his bottom line seems really to have been about calculation:

> Competing on results requires that results be measured and made widely available. Only by measuring and holding every system participant accountable for results will the performance of the health care system ever be significantly improved. . . . *Mandatory measurement and reporting of results is perhaps the single most important step in reforming the health care system.* (Porter and Teisberg, 2006: 6, 7; italics in original)

CATEGORIZATION FOR COMMODIFICATION FOR CALCULATION

Calculation is itself predicated on categorization as well as commodification. You cannot measure what has not been identified— namely, isolated into some unambiguous category. And if what is to be measured in that category is not rather standardized, which pushes it toward being treated as a commodity, then the calculations can become overwhelming—at the limit having to be tailored to each individual case. In other words, calculation is a lot easier when the thing being measured tends toward being a commodity, plus the very act of calculating can encourage it to be seen as a commodity. As Kaplan and Porter put it, their efforts are about "how best to standardize care and treatment processes to reduce the costs of variability" (2011: 12).[1]

Categorization, commodification, and calculation can certainly render the administration of health care easier, and less expensive—for example, in figuring out how to remunerate the providers. That is why governments and insurers alike have been promoting these three Cs for years. But what effect does this have on the quality of services?

It can improve them—sometimes. Getting to know certain health problems well, standardizing the treatments to perfect the execution of them, and collecting systematic evidence on the results have been central to the contemporary practice of medicine. **But does the fact that so many powerful forces in health care—governments, insurers, managers, economists, doctors—line up behind categorization, commodification, and**

[1] While Porter and Teisberg claimed that "health care is anything but a commodity" (2006: 46), how is one to interpret comments related to diseases being identified rather precisely (e.g., prostate cancer as "six different diseases"), treatments of these being isolated from one another (e.g., "medical research reveals that diagnosis and treatments should be increasingly specialized," p. 24), and these being applied in standardized ways (e.g., "providers would charge the same price to any patient for addressing a given medical condition," p. 29)?

calculation make it some sort of administrative panacea? Not at all: these three *C*s need to be recognized for how they hinder as well as help the practices of health care. They hinder where the categories fail, in three respects.

BEYOND, ACROSS, AND BENEATH THE CATEGORIES

"While illnesses are unique, diseases are abstract archetypes relevant to the physician . . . , to the modern hospital administrator, and to insurance providers who rely on diagnostic categories for their spreadsheets and payment schemes" (Fuks, 2009. 5).

Sometimes the categories fit well enough; sometimes they don't. **An illness can fall** *beyond* **the established categories of diseases (i.e., fits none); it can cut** *across* **these categories (i.e., fits several); and much effective treatment requires going** *beneath* **the categories (i.e., the fit alone is insufficient). Add all this up and there is reason to suspect, and not just support, categorization.**

Beyond the Categories

In the index of Porter and Teisberg's book, entitled *Redefining Health Care* (2006), there is no entry for "chronic disease" or "chronic illness" (although there are three under "chronic conditions" and a bunch more under "chronic kidney disease"). Other omissions include mental illness and psychiatry. All of these medical conditions are, of course, relatively difficult to categorize unambiguously and therefore to assess the performance of their treatments. (Witness the unrelenting battles over categories in the DSM—the *Diagnostic and Statistical Manual of Mental Disorders*.) Likewise, as is usual in the field called health care, health promotion and disease prevention get little attention compared with hospitals. These provide the most categorical treatments yet account for only about 30 percent of all expenditures.

This form of oversight is all too common in health care today: slighting whatever falls beyond the established categories, no matter how significant.[2] "Many patients are affected by maladies that have no name yet whose suffering is real" (Fuks, 2009: 6). Bear in mind that beyond the category called disease is the category called illness—what the patient feels compared with what the doctor treats—and beyond that, and patients, is the category called health.[3]

Across the Categories

A second form of oversight can be called *across the categories*. We don't always get conveniently sick; sometimes our illnesses overlap several categories of disease. Even well-defined medical conditions can manifest themselves in multiple and unexpected ways. Forcing round illnesses into the square holes of single diseases has caused its share of problems. Checklists, perhaps the epitome of categorization, may be helpful for much of the practice of medicine, but as Jauhar (2010) put it in reviewing Gawande's book, *The Checklist Manifesto* (2009):

> Checklists may work for managing individual disorders, but it isn't at all clear what to do when several disorders coexist in the same patient, as is often the case with the elderly. And checklists lack flexibility. They might be useful for simple procedures like central line insertion, but they are hardly a

---

[2]Bohmer (2010) distinguished between "rigorously applying scientifically established best practices for diagnosing and treating diseases that are well understood" and those illnesses whose diagnoses are "left largely to the judgment of individual physicians" (pp. 63, 64). For example, in one clinic at Duke University, nurse practitioners apply standard protocol for patients with uncomplicated congenital heart failures "who are responding to treatment as expected," while in another clinic, cardiologists custom treat the complicated cases.

[3]Macmillan cited a professor of cognitive neurophysiology at a Swedish hospital about how "making a commodity out of health care favors those with the easy disorders" (2006).

panacea for the myriad ills of modern medicine. Patients are too varied, their physiologies too diverse and our knowledge still too limited.[4]

Beneath the Categories

Perhaps most significant is oversight beneath the categories. We don't all manifest even our categorically convenient illnesses in the same way. We vary, often in ways that can require significant differences in how we are treated.

This variation can be physiological: my father's appendix appeared in an unusual place, happily found just before it burst. Or it can be psychological, in how we react to how we are "treated." Later we shall discuss various ways in which care and cure interact—for example, care can help cure as well as be cure. Here we reproduce in the accompanying box the striking story of how a particularly caring physician went beneath the category to offer superior service to a patient of his. This box is long, but please read it all, not just as one compelling case, but as an indication of what the very best of medical practice can be.

"It's not easy, you know"
(drawn from Gawande, 2004)

Dr. Warren Warwick, 76 years old, had a particularly high rate of success with his cystic fibrosis patients. The treatments he used, and developed, were the most advanced. They were

---

[4] The problem exists in research too. Groopman offers an interesting criticism of evidence-based medicine, that the clinical trials are typically conducted on patients strictly within the disease categories and so "yield averages that often do not reflect the 'real world' of individual patients, particularly those with multiple medical conditions. Nor do current findings on best practices take into account changes in an illness as it evolves over time" (2010: 4).

well documented and widely followed, yet his performance was remarkably better than other specialists.

Dr. Atul Gawande visited Dr. Warwick to find out why and wrote about it in one of his *New Yorker* articles, entitled "The Bell Curve" (2004). His discovery was obvious yet startling: Dr. Warwick didn't treat his patients in some standardized way: "The secret . . . do whatever you can to keep your patients' lungs as open as possible" (p. 4). That meant going beneath the protocols, to a "combination of focus, aggressiveness, and inventiveness [that made] Dr. Warwick extraordinary. He thinks hard about his patients, he pushes them, and he does not hesitate to improvise" (p. 5).

Gawande's account of Warwick's encounter with one young patient, reproduced below, brings this to life.

> In the clinic one afternoon, I joined [Dr. Warwick] as he saw a seventeen-year-old high-school senior named Janelle, who had been diagnosed with CF at the age of six and had been under his care ever since. She had come for her routine three-month checkup. She wore dyed-black hair to her shoulder blades . . . a stud in her tongue [etc.]. Warwick [in contrast, looked like] a doddering, mid-century academic. He stood in front of Janelle for a moment, hands on his hips, looking her over, and then he said, "So, Janelle, what have you been doing to make us the best CF program in the country?"

> "It's not easy, you know," she said.

> They bantered. She was doing fine. School was going well. Warwick pulled out her latest lung-function measurements. There'd been a slight dip. . . . Three months earlier, Janelle had been at a 109 per cent (she was actually doing better than normal); now she was at around 90 per cent. Ninety per cent was still pretty good, and some ups and downs in the numbers are to be expected. But this was not the way Warwick saw the results.

He knitted his eyebrows. "Why did they go down?" he asked.

Janelle shrugged.

Any cough lately? No. Colds? No. Fevers? No. Was she sure she'd been taking her treatments regularly? Yes, of course. Every day? Yes. Did she ever miss treatments? Sure. Everyone does once in a while. How often is once in a while?

Then, slowly, Warwick got a different story out of her: in the past few months, it turned out, she'd barely been taking her treatments at all.

He pressed on. "Why aren't you taking your treatments?" He appeared neither surprised nor angry. He seemed genuinely curious, as if he'd never run across this interesting situation before.

"I don't know."

He kept pushing. "What keeps you from doing your treatments?"

"I don't know."

"Up here"—he pointed at his own head—"what's going on?"

"I don't know," she said.

He paused for a moment. And then he began speaking to me, taking a new tack. "The thing about patients with CF is that they're good scientists," he said. "They always experiment. We have to help them interpret what they experience as they experiment. So they stop doing their treatments. And what happens? They don't get sick. Therefore, they conclude, Dr. Warwick is nuts."

"Let's look at the numbers," he said to me, ignoring Janelle. He went to a little blackboard he had on the wall. It appeared to be well used. "A person's daily risk of getting a bad lung illness with CF is 0.5 per cent." He wrote the number down. Janelle rolled her eyes. She began tapping her foot.

"The daily risk of getting a bad lung illness with CF plus treatment is 0.05 per cent," he went on, and he wrote that number down. "So when you experiment you're looking at the difference between a 99.95-per-cent chance of staying well and a 99.5-per-cent chance of staying well. Seems hardly any difference, right? On any given day, you have basically a 100-per-cent chance of being well. But"—he paused and took a step toward me—"it is a big difference." He chalked out the calculations. "Sum it up over a year, and it is the difference between an 83-per-cent chance of making it through 2004 without getting sick and only a 16-per-cent chance."

He turned to Janelle. "How do you stay well all your life? How do you become a geriatric patient?" he asked her. Her foot finally stopped tapping. "I can't promise you anything. I can only tell you the odds."

In this short speech was the core of Warwick's world view. He believed that excellence came from seeing, on a daily basis, the difference between being 99.5-per-cent success-ful and being 99.95-per-cent successful. Many activities are like that, of course: catching fly balls, manufacturing microchips, delivering overnight packages. Medicine's only distinction is that lives are lost in those slim margins.

And so he went to work on finding that margin for Janelle. Eventually, he figured out that she had a new boyfriend. She had a new job, too, and was working nights. The boyfriend had his own apartment, and she was either there or at a friend's house most of the time, so she rarely made it home to take her treatments. At school, new rules required her to go to the school nurse for each dose of medicine during the day. So she skipped going. "It's such a pain," she said. He learned that there were some medicines she took and some she didn't. One she took because it was the only thing that she felt actually made a difference. She took her vitamins, too. ("Why your vitamins?" "Because they're cool.") The rest she ignored.

Warwick proposed a deal. Janelle would go home for a breathing treatment every day after school, and get her best friend to hold her to it. She'd also keep key medications in her bag or her pocket at school and take them on her own. ("The nurse won't let me." "Don't tell her," he said, and deftly turned taking care of herself into an act of rebellion.) So far, Janelle was O.K. with this. But there was one other thing, he said: she'd have to come to the hospital for a few days of therapy to recover the lost ground. She stared at him.

"Today?"

"Yes, today."

"How about tomorrow?"

"We've failed, Janelle," he said. "It's important to acknowledge when we've failed."

With that, she began to cry.

But Dr. Warwick did not fail at all; quite the contrary. He was succeeding, by going beneath the categories.[5]

This is certainly a story about categories: cystic fibrosis was the disease; Dr. Warwick's own protocols, the treatment. And it is a story about numbers as well: Dr. Warwick cited them galore—but to support his judgments rather than standardize his practice. He succeeded because he did not commodify the

---

[5] Interestingly, two reviewers of this manuscript reacted to this box in opposite ways. Kristen Herzegh wrote, "Sadly, not a luxury many physicians can take when you consider malpractice, mandated protocols, insurance restrictions." Marie Leinberger wrote, "This type of story is more common than you might think. Doctors and nurses are trained to follow protocols, yes, but there is a huge margin for patient centered care adaptations to those protocols in the real health care world. Patient centered care is the standard at many large teaching institutions for just the reasons you are stating. I don't think this is quite the issue you think it is."

treatment or objectify the patient; he worked with the person beneath the categories, including the category called "patient."[6]

Be the Best? Or Do Your Best?

Porter and Teisberg claimed, "Competition should force providers to equal or exceed the value created by the best provider in their region, the nation, or even internationally" (2006: 47). But with whom was Dr. Warwick competing? Does the phrase "equal or exceed" capture the essence of his success? He was certainly competitive, but mostly against himself: to get better and better.

Was Dr. Warwick exceptional in this regard? Yes and no. Of course, he stood out. But should not every professional stand out by doing his or her best, instead of competing merely to meet or exceed some average, or even to be the best? (Is this not how Michael Porter stands out in his own publications?) Gawande captured this perfectly in concluding his article:

> Somehow, what troubles people isn't so much being average as settling for it. Everyone knows that averageness is, for most of us, our fate. And in certain matters—looks, money, tennis—we would do well to accept this. But in your surgeon, your child's pediatrician, your police department, your local high school? When the stakes are our lives and the lives of our children, we expect averageness to be resisted. And so I push to make myself the best. If I'm not the best already, I believe wholeheartedly that I will be. And you expect that of me, too. Whatever the next round of numbers may say. (p. 7)

So please, bless me with health care providers who, instead of holding their fingers to the wind, be the best they possibly

---

[6] Eight years later Gawande (2012) published a piece called "Big Med" that used the Cheesecake Factory restaurant chain as a model that "represents our best prospect for change" in health care. The article praised "the advantages that size and centralized control [as well as virtual medicine on a screen] can bring." Did Gawande run a draft of this article past Dr. Warwick?

can—do their best while doing good. And if you are an administrator, economist, or even a physician devoted to evidence, please **do your best by getting yourself past the categories of categorization, commodification, and calculation, in order to recognize the significant amount of health care practice, in and out of medicine, that has to be conducted beyond, across, and beneath the standardized categories of your field.**

Beware of the Technocratic Politicians

And, by the way, this should also apply to politicians concerned with health care. In a 2010 article in the *New York Review of Books* entitled "Health Care. Who Knows 'Best'?" Jerome Groopman described a debate in the Obama administration over a socially engineered approach based on "best practices" and "approved standards." As the president put it, "Let's study and figure out what works and what doesn't. And let's encourage doctors and patients to get what works. Let's discourage what doesn't. Let's make sure that our payment incentives allow doctors to do the right thing."

If only the things in question were that simple.

It is interesting how often politicians—left, right, and center, these days it hardly makes any difference—rely on technocratic approaches to governing. (See, for example, Pollock [2004] on Blair in the U.K. and French [1980] on the first Trudeau in Canada.) Is this because so many of them are trained in law, a profession about words (i.e., categories)? Or is it because of where they sit, especially in large nations: removed from the action, and therefore feeling dependent on aggregated statistics?

SOME MYTHS OF MEASUREMENT

"It is a well-known axiom that what is not measured can't be managed" (Kaplan and Porter, in the opening of "How to Solve the Cost Crisis in Health Care," 2011: 4). This is well-known, all right, and false, not to mention downright silly.

Here we have another myth that has been undermining human activities for years, and not only in health care. Education has suffered terribly from an obsession with measurement. To quote from a *New York Times* article entitled "How Measurement Fails Doctors and Teachers" (Wachter, 2016), "We're hitting the targets but missing the point." And in recent years, the same "measurement fatigue" talked about in this article has been damaging many American enterprises, as well as the country's legendary spirit of enterprise (see www.mintzberg .org/enterprise).

Who ever successfully measured culture, leadership, even the potential for a truly new product? Can none of these thus be managed? Did Kaplan and Porter measure the effectiveness of their own recommendations? **Indeed, who has even tried to measure the performance of measurement itself, aside from assuming that it is marvelous?** And how about measuring the performance of management? (Don't tell me that increase in share price does this for CEOs.) I guess, therefore, measurement and management can't be managed.

Many of the things that matter most in organizations (and in life, for that matter) cannot be measured. Yet they do somehow have to be managed, whether personally or organizationally. **Certainly we have to measure what we can; we just cannot allow ourselves to be mesmerized by measurement—which we so often are.**

In my opinion, *mesmerization by* the numbers has become an even greater problem than *manipulation of* the numbers. As a physician wrote recently: "I am in an ongoing struggle with those who ignore or discount everything they cannot measure."

Why so? A senior civil servant in a large health ministry explained, after a fashion, "What else can we do when we don't understand what's going on?" How about leaving your office to find out what's going on? It's not so hard. David Behan, at the time director-general of Social Care (for people with physical disabilities, learning disabilities, and so on) in the English Department of Health, told our health care management class (imhl.org) that he was spending his Friday afternoons in the field, preferring to speak with the users of the services without the professionals, the professionals without the managers, and the managers by themselves. He described his job as "not to tell them what to do" but "to help them find their own way."

The medical profession is hardly immune to all this. The buzzword for clinicians these days is "evidence-based medicine." Good doctors are supposed to rely on the numbers of proper research to justify their interventions—not their own judgment or experience so much as the correct evidence.

Yet when we asked the participants in our International Masters for Health Leadership program, most of them physicians, to map their practice between evidence and experience, they put themselves all over the place, most in-between, but tilted toward experience. One commented, "I see evidence as part of my experience," and another talked about "the tyranny of evidence." The best comment was that it should be called "evidence-*guided* medicine." Labels are not casual. (We have already discussed the person beyond the "patient"; later we shall discuss "alternate" forms of practice—why alternate?)

According to Gawande (2004), Dr. Warwick, who had such success with his cystic fibrosis patients, was "almost contemptuous of established findings," which he saw as "a record of the past and little more." Gawande added, "We are used to thinking that a doctor's ability depends mainly on science and skill. The lesson [here] is that these may be the easiest parts of care ... more nebulous factors like aggressiveness and consistency and ingenuity can matter enormously." These days everyone is being graded, including "firemen, CEOs, and salesmen." But the grades "never seem to measure the right things" (p. 6; for CEO performance in business, see my commentary "No More Executive Bonuses" [2009b]).

Porter and Teisberg wrote, "What is needed is competition on results, not just evidence-based medicine" (2006: 7). That way users would have a basis to choose among hospitals and physicians, also "providers would charge the same price to any patient for addressing a given medical condition" (p. 29).

But what is so *given* about the medical conditions that fall beyond, across, and beneath the categories? **Must every condition be conveniently slotted into a pigeonhole for the convenience of calculation, in the hope that it will fit?** Given his results, patients would certainly choose Dr. Warwick. But his treatment was not given, nor was the young woman he was treating. He was customizing the treatment to her as a person.

The easiest thing to measure, and to price, would have been the amount of time he spent with her—which is precisely the problem. A hospital administrator or government official might well have asked, "Why is he spending so much time with this one patient? Maybe she'll live longer with that kind of attention, but it will be years before we know that, and now we have budgets to meet."

How often have hospitals, insurers, and health ministries punished the Dr. Warwicks of this world for spending too much time with their patients, by treating them as people? **Because economics begins before medicine ends, the technocrats of health care have too often trumped the professionals.**[7]

---

[7]"Actual duration should be calculated for time-consuming, less predictable processes, especially those that involve multiple physicians and nurses performing complex care activities such as major surgery or examination of patients with complicated medical circumstances" (Kaplan and Porter, 2011: 9). This is reminiscent of a comment in a South African newspaper that "a long-range weather forecast should be obtained before leaving, as weather conditions are extremely unpredictable" (*Natal Daily News*, June 15, 1982). See the discussion later on "Analyst, Analyze Thyself."

So what is the conscientious administrator who cannot just rely on measurement to do? That's easy. **Use judgment. Not exclusively, just appropriately.**

Remember Judgment?

Do you remember judgment? After all, dictionaries still include the word. Of course I mean informed judgment, by wise people. But is there any other form that deserves the label? Wise people see and experience for themselves, yet appreciate the limitations of that, and so strive to extend their knowledge as much as possible—including allowing themselves to be guided by reliable evidence as well as successful experience. They judge the people, the situation, the advice, and the numbers, too, just as they use the numbers to check out their judgments.

Evidence has to be put in its place—namely, where it can aid judgment, not replace it. There are times when the evidence is so weak that professionals have to rely on judgment, based on experience. But never is the evidence so strong that they can afford to suspend judgment. Our world is only as good as the judgment of the people in places of significance.[8]

The next section addresses the overt limitations of measurement, and the section after that considers what is probably the most covert bias of measurement.

The Soft Underbelly of Hard Data

Numbers are precise, so people assume they are reliable. This can be dangerous.

---

[8] Hippocrates apparently claimed that the most difficult aspect of medical practice is in the exercise of judgment. That has yet to change. "Life is short, and the Art long; the occasion fleeting; experience fallacious, and judgment difficult. The physician must not only be prepared to do what is right himself, but also to make the patient, the attendants, and externals cooperate."

We talk about "hard data" (even when in "soft copy"). Rocks are hard; data are not. Most data have a decidedly soft underbelly. So be careful of them, for several reasons (from Mintzberg, 1975, 2013: 124–126):

First, hard data are limited in scope. They may provide the basis for description but not for explanation. OK, so 62 percent of the patients got better. Why? What about the rest? (Read later about how one of the great discoveries of medicine, that cholera was transmitted by water, not air, came about because of two outliers in an otherwise tight sample.) Understanding requires getting past the numbers, to the specific case (as did Dr. Warwick). In contrast, one of the subjects of Kinsey's famous study of sexual behavior in the human male afterward complained bitterly of the insult to his masculine ego: "No matter what I told him, he just looked me straight in the eye and asked 'How many times?'" (in Kaplan 1964: 171).

Second, hard data are often overly aggregated. Happenings generate facts that are combined and then reduced to some number, such as that quintessential bottom line. Think of how much information is lost in the process. Health care deals mostly with the lives of single people: it shouldn't allow anyone to drown in a lake whose average depth is six inches.

Switching metaphors, it is fine to see the forest from the trees—unless you are in the lumber business. Too much managing takes place as if from a helicopter, where the trees look like a green carpet. As Neustadt commented in his study of presidents of the United States, they needed "not the bland amalgams . . . [but] the tangible detail that pieced together in [their] mind illuminate the underside of issues put before [them]" (1960: 153, 154). Likewise, as described in the accompanying box, hospitals cannot count livers the way McDonald's counts hamburgers.

Counting Livers
(based on a story recounted by Sholom Glouberman)

A liver transplant surgeon in London, England operated on 10 people. Eight survived the operation. Of these, a previous cancer reappeared in one, and she was not expected to survive. The new liver of another failed and he needed a second transplant. Of the remaining six, three were too sick to resume work.

The surgeon was asked about his success rate: 8 out of 10, he replied, and it could be 9 out of 11 after that second operation. (He counted livers, not people.) An immunologist said 7 out of 10, because he believed the surgeon should not have operated on the woman who had the cancer. The managers of the hospital said 6 out of 10, while the nurses, who knew the patients best, said 3 out of 10. And the right answer is . . . .

Where is the magic envelope for those who have to decide about continuing this procedure?

Third, hard data can arrive too late. Even good information takes time to "harden." Don't be fooled by the speed of those electrons racing around the Internet. Events and results first have to be documented as "facts" and then aggregated into reports, which may have to await some predetermined schedule.

Fourth, a surprising amount of hard data is just plain unreliable. Lift up the rock over hard data and see what you find crawling underneath:

> Public agencies are very keen on amassing statistics—they collect them, add them, raise them to the nth power, take the cube root and prepare wonderful diagrams. But what you must never forget is that every one of those figures comes in

the first instance from the village watchman, who just puts down what he damn pleases (attributed to Sir Josiah Stamp, 1928, cited in Maltz 1997).

Who goes back to find out what the watchmen put down, for example, in the hospitals where the nurses and doctors are constantly being interrupted by administrative engineering? Moreover, recorded facts that were reliable in the first instance can lose something in the quantification. Numbers get rounded up; nuances get lost; mistakes get made. Anyone who has ever produced a quantitative measure knows just how much distortion is possible, intentional as well as unintentional.

Moreover, outputs are different from outcomes: success depends on *what* is measured, and how. Remember Vioxx, and so many other medications that began with good numbers? Are you in need of a really good surgeon for a difficult operation? Let me suggest you ask about these with high death rates, because they may be dealing with the toughest cases.[9]

In 1950, Ely Devons published a remarkable study on the use of hard data in the British Air Ministry during World War II. His findings were hardly encouraging. The collection of such data was extremely difficult and subtle, demanding "a high degree of skill," yet it "was treated ... as inferior, degrading and routine work on which the most inefficient clerical staff could best be employed" (p. 134). Errors entered the data in all kinds of ways, even just treating months as normal although all included some holiday or other. "Figures were often merely a useful way of summing up judgment and guesswork." Sometimes the figures were "developed through 'statistical bargaining'. But

---

[9] An article appeared in the *New York Times* on July 22, 2015, entitled "Giving Doctors Grades" (Jauhar, 2015). It reported that surgical "report cards" had in some cases backfired, penalizing those who treated very sick patients, and that some surgeons were even "cherry picking" their patients, and "declin[ing] to treat more difficult and complicated patients."

once a figure was put forward . . . no one was able by rational argument to demonstrate that it was wrong." And "when those figures were called 'statistics,' they acquired the authority and sanctity of Holy Writ" (p. 155).

"Efficiency" Reduced to Economy

To conclude this discussion and fully appreciate what can go wrong with measurement, consider the word efficiency (drawn from Mintzberg [1982, also 1989: Chap. 6]). Efficiency has been described by Herbert Simon (1950: 14), winner of one of those erroneously labeled Nobel Prizes in Economics,[10] as a "completely neutral" concept—getting, as the saying goes, the greatest bang for the buck, whatever bang it is you want. By this description, surely health care needs more bangs for its bucks—to become more efficient. Who can be against that?

Me, for one. Consider efficiency in use. A restaurant is efficient. To what am I referring? (Stop and think of one thing.) And my house is efficient. (Again.)

Did you think of speed of service in the restaurant, the cost of heating in the house? I have asked these questions of many groups, and most people (English speaking at least; the word has a different connotation in some other languages) think of these two. Why? How often do you choose a restaurant because of the speed of its service, compared with the quality of its food? And who ever bought a house because of its fuel efficiency, instead of its look or proximity to good schools, etc.? Can so many people be so inefficient? Technically, yes; practically, no.

Do you realize what is happening? **When people use the word** *efficiency,* **they zero in** *subconsciously* **on the characteristic that can most easily be measured. And so, too, unfortunately, do**

---

[10] Alfred Nobel never created a prize in economics. This prize was created by the Bank of Sweden, designated to be in Nobel's memory. (See http://www .mintzberg.org/blog/there-is-no-nobel-prize-economics-and-why-it-matters.)

many managers, economists, accountants, and administrative engineers in pursuit of efficiency (and of productivity, too: see www.mintzberg.org/enterprise), not to mention that MBA student who studied the symphony orchestra. **In a world where not everything can equally be measured, a focus on efficiency deflects attention away from much that matters. This is especially so in health care** (and education as well). That is because

a. Costs are usually easier to measure than benefits. Compare the savings from cutting the nursing staff with its effects on the quality of care.

b. Economic costs are usually easier to measure than social costs. Compare the savings above with the wear and tear on the nurses who remain.[11]

c. Economic benefits are usually easier to measure than social benefits. And so doctors are usually paid for the quantity of their throughput, not the quality of their treatments.

Thus, **what people call** *efficiency* **all too often reduces to** *economy*, **more specifically to** *economizing*: **cutting tangible costs at the expense of intangible benefits.**[12] Let's take an example right here. You are reading this book. How much is it costing you? That's easy: so much money to buy, so many hours to read. Now please quantify the benefits of reading this book.

------

[11] Economists have a convenient word for the social costs that can be sloughed off because they are not easily measured, and so not easily attributable to whoever created them: *externalities*. This includes the garbage we send down the chute, the air we pollute with our cars, the breakdown in the families of the people we "downsize" in our companies. The problem with externalities is that they are destroying our world.

[12] See Head on how "The New Ruthless Economy" does this in health care, for example, by having physicians swipe cards to control their time with patients, using "telephone triage" to restrict patients' access to them before it comes to that, and speeding up the training of physicians in the first place (2003: 126–128).

Good luck. You may be reveling in its illustrious insights yet never do a thing with any of them. Or you may be reviling every word (why are you still reading?) yet years from now make some significant change because of something you forgot you read here. So, should you stop reading now for want of measurable benefits? If so, you will have to stop all reading—indeed, much of your living, too. Think of how efficient you will become!

Think about quality, too, in restaurants and elsewhere. Pirsig (1974) wrote a popular book called *Zen and the Art of Motorcycle Maintenance,* about how quality cannot be defined (let alone measured), yet we know it when we see it. But do those administrators who sacrifice quality to cut costs see it in the reports they read in their offices?

Some years ago, the government of Canada cut its funding to the national Medicare program. The economic savings showed up immediately, and quantitatively—on the government's budgetary bottom line. But the effects on the quality of health care took years to reveal themselves, and then more in anecdotes than statistics—for example, in the death of someone waiting in an overcrowded emergency room. Eventually this reached crisis proportions, so money was put back in (by the same person, as prime minister, who had taken it out as finance minister).

And how about all those governments around the world that saved so much money by closing hospitals for the mentally ill and leaving them to roam the streets? All this was very efficient, too: save now, pay later. (Actually we pay now, but only realize it later.) **It requires no great intelligence to cut costs, only to do so without undermining quality.**

An article by three McKinsey consultants, entitled "Private Solutions for Health Care in the Gulf" (Hediger et al., 2007), discussed favorably one country where "private companies are invited to bid on how much less funding they could accept while still meeting specified standards of quality and service." Another country gave certain contracts to the winning bidder with "total operating freedom but also full accountability for performance" (p. 55). It sounds fine, but did anyone ever check on how reliably specified were those "standards of quality," and how "full" was that accountability?

Governments and insurers tie themselves in knots trying to measure such things. And when they fail, they have a simple solution: more measurement. Find fancier, more elaborate numbers. The popular *balanced scorecard* (Kaplan and Norton, 1992) assumes that the game of measurement is played on a field leveled between the economic team on one side and the social team on the other. Play for the latter and discover how tilted that field really is.

So it is time to face the music. **Measurement can be fine, so long as it is used sensibly. But too often, in management and sometimes medicine as well, it is used mindlessly. Health care needs to become more effective by getting less efficient.**

ANALYST, ANALYZE THYSELF

Back to measuring the consequences of measurement. The United States spends something like 31 percent of its health care dollars on administration. The administrative engineers and other analysts would have it spend more, albeit to reduce the other 69 percent. Is that a reasonable investment?

Don't look to these analysts for the answer. They are about the costs of delivering health care, not the costs of analyzing it—costs incurred by everyone else, not themselves.

In their article "How to Solve the Cost Crisis in Health Care," Kaplan and Porter (2011) provide a list of seven steps "to estimate the total costs of treating . . . patient populations":

1. Select the medical condition [specifying the possible "complications and comorbidities" (i.e., the presence of multiple disorders)].

2. Define the care delivery value chain ... which charts the principal activities [associated with the condition].
3. Develop process maps for each activity ... the paths patients may follow. ...
4. Obtain time estimates for each process.
5. Estimate the cost of supplying patient care resources.
6. Estimate the capacity of each resource and calculate the capacity cost rate.
7. Calculate the total cost of patient care. (pp. 8–12)

Don't look for:

8. Include the costs of doing all this.

But you can get a sense of it by reading the authors' example of a knee replacement, for which 77 activities are listed.[13] Multiply this by elbows, hips, brains, hearts and minds, etc., factor in the frequency of improvements in these activities, one by one, and you have to wonder if analysts will soon outnumber clinicians in health care.

But the direct costs of their efforts are not the only costs. How about the costs of the distractions to the clinicians—for example, by having to record so much data—plus the costs of the political battles that ensue over who is measuring what, how, where, when, and for whom. Analysts see measurements as objective; contrast this with the political blood spilled over determining them.

Years ago, the British retailer Marks and Spencer decided it was spending too much money controlling the movement of stock in its stores. So instead of a clerk filling out an order form to replenish a shelf, which was handed to another clerk behind

---

[13] Not to mention that "outcomes for any medical condition or patient population should be measured along multiple dimensions, including survival, ability to function, duration of care, discomfort and complications, and the sustainability of recovery" (p. 5).

a counter, who went to fetch the items, etc., the company got rid of the whole procedure and simply let the clerks go in the back and scoop up what they needed. The company was able to function with thousands fewer clerks and 26 million fewer cards and papers (Howey, 1993). Now that's truly efficient—and a vote of faith in the honesty of the clerks. Health care administrators take note: treated with respect, left to figure many things out for themselves, health care professionals may prove to be as trustworthy as store clerks.

Myth #6

The health care system can be fixed with increased competition.

Whether or not health care is a business or should be run like one (to be discussed next), there is the claim that it can be improved with increased levels of competition. I shall challenge this on the following grounds: first, that **in the United States, where competition is probably the greatest and so too are these beliefs, competition has likely done more harm than good in health care;** and second, that **health care, everywhere, already has too much competition, but of a kind less recognized—it requires a great deal more cooperation.** Along the way, I will also note that the case for competition is largely about individualization.

IS AMERICAN COMPETITION THE MODEL?

The United States has a love affair with competition, and so it should: competition has been good for many things, such as computers and cars. But has it been good for health care? Of course it has: some competition is always good. It keeps people from becoming complacent, challenging them to do better. But how much competition is required, especially in a field where the professionals have to do *their own best*?

In the U.S. the answer looks to be: too much. This country that so favors competition has the most expensive health care costs in the world, by far—at least double per capita most of its counterparts—with average outcomes that are hardly good. On preventable deaths (meaning before age 75, amenable to treatment), in 2014, the Commonwealth Fund reported the U.S. ranking last among the industrialized countries (based on 2006 statistics). In France, for example, the rate in 2011 was half that of the U.S.[1]

In many respects Canada is much like the U.S. Before it introduced public Medicare across the board in the 1960s, the two countries had comparable figures. Since then, American costs have soared way ahead of those in Canada—in 2013, $9,086 per capita compared with $4,569—while Canadian outcomes have surpassed those of the United States (on the latter, see Dressel, 2006).[2]

---

[1] Summarizing several surveys and studies, with data on Canada, Germany, the Netherlands, New Zealand, the U.K., and the U.S., Davis et al. (2010) found that "the U.S. health care system ranks last or next-to-last on five dimensions of a high performance health system: quality, access, efficiency, equity, and healthy lives." The last WHO ranking (in 2000) put the United States 37th in "overall health system performance."

[2] Some of these outcomes can be attributed to inequalities in American health care, especially concerning the uninsured, although that hardly justifies them. But even for the insured, the risk of going bankrupt due to the high costs remain. As for longevity, some have argued that this is a consequence of lifestyle (smoking, obesity, etc. [Tierney, 2009]), as if health promotion and disease prevention are not part of health care—or, with respect to our discussion here, that these are not connected to the competitive nature of American society.

Crucially, we haven't addressed the structural perversities that are driving the health care system to bankruptcy. Obamacare or no Obamacare, American health care is still distorted by the fee-for-service system that rewards quantity over quality and creates a gigantic incentive for inefficiency and waste. (Brooks, 2012b)

Putting all this together, **shall we take America's performance as a testimonial to the wonders of competition in health care?**[3] Not putting it together, many American experts have done just that:

Government control smothers competition under a blanket of uniformity, but it is competition that will improve the quality of health care service and will create the best opportunities for cost control. Consumer-driven entrepreneurs will compete to offer the best health promotion strategies, the best health care services, and the best technology by creating more for less. This kind of competition ultimately controls costs and raises quality. (Herzlinger, 2007: 142)[4]

In American health care? How about a little evidence? If you always do as you always did, you will always get what you always got. Well, not quite: Americans are getting less for more.[5]

---

[3] See Sibley (1995) on "The Hyperthyroid Economy," about an obsession with competition equivalent to excessive thyroid imbalance in the human body.
[4] After the 1960s, the "reform-minded experts [in the U.S.] ... increasingly left behind public-interest ideals and their underlying extra-market values in favor of organizing and improving health care markets" (Melhado, 2006: 359).
[5] And that might include the rich, who have always been seen as getting the best of health care. A 2006 study found that the rates of diabetes and heart disease among the wealthiest and best-educated Americans were comparable with those of the poorest and least-educated English (Banks et al., 2006 as cited by Greene, 2006). Is this a matter of lifestyle rather than medical services? Perhaps, partly, but if so, blame American health promotion and disease prevention.

PORTER AND TEISBERG ON THE "RIGHT KIND" OF COMPETITION

In their *Harvard Business Review* article entitled "Redefining Competition in Health Care" (2004), followed by their 2006 book, Porter and Teisberg, while acknowledging that American health care is "subject to more competition than virtually anyplace else in the world," pleaded for more competition, but of "the right kind"—namely, "at the level of diseases or treatments." They described this as having the potential to become "the engine of progress and reform" that will "unleash a tidal wave of improvements in quality and efficiency" (2004: 21, 27, 30).[6]

The authors refer to the old kind of competition as "zero sum," which they characterized as "too broad" in terms of the range of services provided (especially in hospitals), "too narrow" and "unintegrated" within service lines (being based on specialized medical treatments instead of the full cycle of care), and "too localized" on geographic bases (volumes too small for specific interventions that impede the ability of providers to be truly excellent [2004, 2006: 151]). Add this together and you get one of Porter and Teisberg's prime recommendations: to favor larger, less local, and more specialized practices and hospitals.[7]

---

[6] A number of the major problems of competition in U.S. health care are dismissed by Porter and Teisberg. About the huge costs of lawsuits, for example, which the authors describe as raising costs without benefits to the patients (with less than 30 percent of the payments for malpractice insurance ending up with them or their families), they claim that "with better information and no restrictions on choice, many lawsuits will be averted" (2004: 31). Their solution to the problem of deep discounts for large patient populations amounts to much the same kind of dismissal (p. 25).

[7] It might be helpful to understand where Porter is coming from. His field is business strategy, particularly the locating of enterprises in sustainable strategic positions, for example, by offering differentiated products, or concentrating on low costs, or focusing on specific markets (see his book *Competitive Strategy*, 1980). General hospitals do not have such strategic focus; they are

What will the health care system look like when all participants focus on patient value? Providers will offer services where they can be truly excellent, rather than attempting to offer all services to every patient. Care will be organized around medical conditions and coordinated across the cycle of care.... Fewer providers will offer care for each medical condition, but the care they offer will be far more integrated.... Today's duplicative and excess capacity will be significantly reduced. A growing number of excellent regional and national providers will operate across multiple geographic areas, linked to local institutions through various types of medical partnerships and relationships. (2004: 382–383)

A little utopian, perhaps?

Specialized hospitals—what Herzlinger called "focused factories" (2007: 168–172)—do of course exist, for cataracts and hernias, etc.[8] That makes sense, where applicable, which is less than what is implied by these authors. Many hospital services need to be available locally—for example, in obstetrics—and sometimes also in the same institution—for example, emergency services, so that patients can be transferred conveniently to medical specialties. Many illnesses cut across disease categories and so require different specialists in the same place. Geriatric and other patients often cannot be transferred out of town without aggravating their conditions and upsetting their families. In other words, **in much of health care and beyond just hospitals, community matters, even if it gets little attention in**

---

differentiated by geographic location, and so do not seem to be very strategic from Porter's perspective. But need they be?

[8] Sholom Glouberman has suggested that Porter, Teisberg, and Herzlinger, all from the Harvard Business School, may have been overly influenced by the school's case study of the Shouldice Clinic in Toronto, which for years has been specialized in hernia operations. Ironically, although privately owned, it now does most of its work on contract to public Medicare in Ontario.

mainstream economics. (In Porter and Teisberg's book, called *Redefining Health Care*, the focus is on hospitals and diseases, not on community care or public health.)

Certainly the authors' plea to focus on the medical condition in its "full cycle" is better than a focus on single treatments. But shouldn't the real focus of health care be on the care of health, not just the treatment of disease, and on the person as more than a patient?

DOES COMPETITION NECESSARILY FOSTER INNOVATION?

For Porter and Teisberg, this question is almost rhetorical:

> In a normal market, competition drives relentless improvements in quality and cost. Rapid innovation leads to rapid diffusion of new technologies and better ways of doing things. Excellent competitors prosper and grow, while weaker rivals are restructured or go out of business. Quality-adjusted prices fall, value improves, and the market expands to meet the needs of more consumers (2006: 3)

Of course competition can foster innovation. Just look at Apple, Google, Amazon. But always? Can it not sometimes sap innovation?

Consider the pharmaceutical companies. They certainly compete on research, to be the first with some new blockbuster drug. And they have had their noticeable successes. Yet, as discussed earlier, we also know that research in some of the largest of these companies has been faltering in recent years. In my 2006 article called "Patent Nonsense," I drew attention to some of this:

> A 2003 article in the *New York Times* reported that "9 top scientists" had recently left GlaxoSmithKline because they

believed "its laboratory productivity was getting worse, not better. 'It's a disaster,' said one of them, Dr. Peter G. Taber, who was the company's chief of clinical development until February." He added: "The effect of mergers on research productivity is an issue that this industry has yet to deal with" (Harris, 2003). A 2004 article in the *Financial Times* (Bowe and Dyer, 2004) about Pfizer, the company that had been most heavily engaged in mergers, claimed "that while it was out deal-making, its own research dried-up." (2006b: 374)

What were the greatest pharmaceutical breakthroughs of the 20th century? Stop here for a moment and make your own short list.

If you named penicillin (leading to antibiotics), insulin for diabetics, or Salk vaccine for polio, you should know that all three came out of not-for-profit laboratories. With whom was Alexander Fleming competing when he realized that the fungus contaminating some of his cultures could be used to treat disease? (Picture Fleming sitting in front of a screen in some pharmaceutical company today, reviewing millions of molecules.)

Of course, there are the stories of celebrated scientists who competed with one another to be first with some grand discovery (as told about the finding of the double helix—which, by the way, also came out of a not-for-profit laboratory). Less celebrated, but hardly less common, are the stories of cooperation among scientists, who built on each other's ideas (as did Crick with Watson, if not exactly with Franklin, in making that discovery).

And how about the suppression of research findings between competing scientists? Does that promote innovation, or slow it down? The answer is yes both times, depending on the circumstances. There is the incentive to beat others, but also the failure to build on each other's findings. (Watson and Crick, by the way, were able to build on Franklin's findings, despite their mutual suspicions.)[9] **So competition is no more a panacea in health care than is cooperation. We need both. It is worth reiterating here that the most talented people succeed by doing *their* best.**[10]

Markets can be wonderful. Believe me, I appreciate having my choice of restaurants and automobile companies. If they don't serve me well, I go elsewhere. I appreciate having my choice of physicians too. But do the latter serve me well because they live in mortal fear that I will take my "business" elsewhere?

---

[9]Consider this passage from Longman's book on the Veterans Administration, where he compared the IT system in two hospitals:

> The system that Midland adopted is based on software originally written by doctors for doctors at the VA. It is, with a few qualifications we need not bother with, "open-source" software, meaning the code can be read and modified by anyone and is freely available in the public domain rather than copyrighted by a corporation. For nearly thirty years ... the VA software's code has been continually improved by a large community of collaborating, computer-minded health-care professionals, at first within the VA and later at medical institutions around the world ...

> The software Children's Hospital installed, by contrast, was the product of a private company called Cerner Corporation. It was designed by software engineers using locked, proprietary code that medical professionals were barred from seeing, let alone modifying. ... While a few large institutions have managed to make meaningful use of proprietary programs, these systems have just as often led to gigantic cost overruns and sometimes life-threatening failures. (2012: 113–114)

[10]David Brooks (2012a) claimed in one of his *New York Times* columns that "we tend to confuse capitalism with competition." Quoting Peter Thiel, he referred to establishing "a creative monopoly" where "everybody has to come to you. ... Creative people don't follow the crowds; they seek out the blank spots on the map ... the wilderness nobody knows. ... You don't have to compete; you can invent."

IS THIS REALLY ABOUT COMPETITION?

Is all this concern about competition really about competition? Let's take a closer look at that competition.

Consider those specialized hospitals favored by Porter and Teisberg. Are they necessarily more competitive? It can be argued that the more they specialize, the less they compete, at least with each other. After all, how many hospitals devoted to hernias can any region support? Likewise in business, a good deal of the competing is intended to suppress competition—for example, by merging with competitors, creating cartels, lobbying governments for tariff protection, and so on [11]

And then there is competition as a race to the bottom—for example, when pharmaceutical companies bribe physicians with gifts and when they bias research findings by funding it.

---

[11] It is telling that in his book *Competitive Strategy*, Porter (1980) had a section on strategies to consolidate a fragmented industry but no comparable section on strategies to fragment a consolidated industry (preferred by entrepreneurs). His bias has been for size, scale, and that often means less competition, not more. The words "politics" and "power" do not appear in the index or table of contents of this book, but it does not require a leap of imagination to see it as a primer on the use of corporate power and politics to suppress competition. Read about "barriers to entry," the use of lawsuits as a strategy against "weaker firms" (p. 80), etc. (For more on this, see Mintzberg et al. [1998, 2009: Chap. 4]; also Kennedy and Pomerantz [1986]). "Porter focused strategy on how to protect business from other business rivals. The goal of strategy . . . was to find a safe haven for businesses from the destructive forces of competition" (Denning, 2012). Porter and Teisberg claim that they "are mindful of the possibility that some providers will respond to results competition by trying to game the system to manipulate their numbers. However, competition will also create a strong motivation to expose manipulation, while advancing results measures and risks adjustment methodologies that make manipulation difficult. Results competition is sure to trigger an intense and sorely needed discussion about how to measure and compare results fairly" (2006: 104). But where is the evidence for that? In the business world today, evidence to the contrary is ubiquitous, most of it coming directly out of competing from results: to get a bottom line that will impress the stock market analysts.

All of this is hardly what Porter and Teisberg want. But it is what all of us often get. In health care, this can be particularly insidious, not only because it can involve matters of life and death, but also because **caveat emptor (let the buyer beware) can become awfully crass in a field like health care, when the seller knows an awful lot more than the buyer.**

THE COST OF COMPETITION

An article in the *New York Times* attributed the high costs of U.S. health care to excessive competition: "Duplicate processing of claims, large numbers of insurance products, complicated bill paying systems and high marketing costs [plus all the "paperwork required of American doctors and hospitals that simply doesn't exist in countries like Canada or Britain"] add up to huge administrative expenses" (Bernasek, 2006). Consider a vivid case in point:

> A situation . . . occurred in the emergency room with a [woman] who came in at four a.m. suffering from an upper-gastrointestinal bleed. . . . This patient was a member of an H.M.O. The physician called for a gastroenterologist to perform an emergency procedure to stop the bleeding. The gastroenterologist would not treat the patient without a prior authorization from the insurance company, knowing that if he did not receive authorization, he would not be paid for performing the procedure. The doctor tried to contact the insurance company for over an hour to receive authorization. In the meantime, the emergency room had to give this patient four units of blood, which otherwise would not have been administered if the procedure had been done. When it looked as if this patient might not live . . . the doctor called again to the insurance company and told them if he did not receive authorization he would be contacting the *Las Vegas*

Review-Journal with this story. The insurance company then authorized the gastroenterologist to perform the procedure to stop the bleeding. (Hitchens, 1998: 66)

Gordon Best, an American who has lived in England for many years where he has advised numerous senior officials in health care, has claimed that in the United States, "It is . . . clear that having competing payers complicates the market, massively, and increases transaction and overhead costs but does not appear to do much for outcomes or responsiveness to patients" (2007: 11).

So what are we to make of all this competition? Is American health care simply in a competitive mess? Yes, significantly so. Thus the solution is staring the country in the face. "No one is in charge," wrote Harris (2004) in the *New York Times* about the problems caused by drug shortages. And who might be in charge? If you are an American enamored with competitive markets, cover your eyes when you get to the answer proposed at the end of the next myth.

COOPERATION, NOT INDIVIDUALIZATION

Of course, we are all competitive beings, from which can spring good and bad. But all of us are also cooperative beings, from which can spring a lot more good. This is especially so in health care.

I refer here not just to market competition for the recipients of the services, but also to all the individuals and institutions vying for more resources of every kind. Think of the political battles that consume so much effort: physicians competing with one another for more beds, and hospitals maneuvering around one another for larger budgets. This is understandable to a point, but in health care that point is too often surpassed. And with so much of the powerful health care establishment lined up on the side of treating diseases, no wonder that the promotion of health and the prevention of illness get so little attention. Competition favors whoever has the power. Especially but not only in America, **in the name of competition, health care suffers from individualization: every user, every provider, every service, every institution, every region for his-, her-, or itself.**

Porter and Teisberg wrote, "At its most basic level, competition in health care must take place where value is actually created" (2006: 5). Replace the word *competition* with *cooperation* and reread this sentence, to make it more compelling. To sum up: **What the field of health care desperately needs is not more or other kinds of competition so much as a great deal more coordination, cooperation, and collaboration.**

7

Myth #7

Health care organizations can be fixed by managing them more like businesses.

When it comes to managing everything, this is a prevailing myth in our societies, especially the U.S, that business has it right while most other institutions, especially government, have it wrong. Therefore, all must ape business, if not actually become businesses.

Across government services, this agenda has been promoted as the "New Public Management," which is a euphemism for old corporate practices (Mintzberg, 1996). As a consequence, **much of the public sector now ambles about like an amnesiac, pretending to be business.** When an official of the George W. Bush White House staff was questioned in 2002 on a belated start to a propaganda offensive for action against Iraq, he replied, "From a marketing point of view, you don't introduce new products in August." War had become a new product! When that administration named its secretary of the army, he promised to bring in "sound business practice." He came from Enron, just before its spectacular collapse.

It is time to make the opposite case: that **management as now practiced in much of the corporate world is no longer good even for business, let alone for health care and many other social and public services.** (See www.mintzberg.org/enterprise; also Chap. 4 of my book *Managers Not MBAs* [2004].) That is because so much of it relies on myths of its own: that people are human resources (I am a human being); that managers can be created in an MBA classroom (hubris yes, but managers?); that leadership is somehow superior to management (try leading without managing); that strategies can be planned at the "top" for "implementation" at the bottom ("top" is a distorting metaphor: strategies are learned, not planned [Mintzberg, 1989]); and that organizations are about charts and mission statements (anybody working in a hospital who needs a mission statement should find a job somewhere else). All of this is undermining businesses themselves, but not as fast as the health care organizations that are imitating them.

We are taught to think that big government is bureaucratic. Ask people who work in big business about that. (Better still, read Dilbert.) It is no coincidence that the two most popular techniques in the history of management, time and motion studies to control employees' hands and strategic planning systems to control their heads, have been embraced most enthusiastically by communist governments and western corporations.

HERZLINGER ON THIS BUSINESS OF HEALTH CARE

Porter and Teisberg referred repeatedly to health care as a business, at one point urging the adoption of certain practices as "in most businesses" (2004: 28). But their Harvard Business School colleague Regina Herzlinger (2006; see also her 2007 book *Who Killed Health Care?*) went further. Aside from repeatedly calling health care a "business," she also referred to "one-stop shopping" for health care; to hospitals as "focused factories" (2006: 59); to the "customers" and "consumers of health care" for whom "the passive [term] 'patient' seems anarchistic"; and to physicians as "industry players" (p. 61).[1]

Herzlinger's article is entitled "Why Innovation in Health Care Is So Hard." This is a curious title given the impressive record of innovation in medicine. She did acknowledge this but then moved quickly to her concern: not the development of health care but "the packaging and delivery" of those treatments, many of which she called "consumer unfriendly" (p. 1).

In other words, in her view it is the administration of health care that has lacked the innovation, a conclusion with which I obviously concur. But how Herzlinger's proposed solution—treating health care more like a business—can be considered innovative is beyond me. In the United States, it amounts to pouring more of the usual oil on the fires of health care.

Atul Gawande, the physician who writes regularly on health care for the *New Yorker,* discussed one particularly corrupt town in Texas where "a medical community came to see patients the way subprime-mortgage lenders saw home buyers: as profit centers"—namely providers of "a revenue stream" (2009a: 14, 12):

> They instruct their secretary to have patients who call with follow-up questions schedule an appointment, because insurers don't pay for phone calls, only office visits. They consider providing Botox injections for cash. They take a Doppler ultrasound course, buy a machine, and start doing

---

[1] Head (2003: 135) has traced the origin of the health maintenance organizations (HMOs, discussed earlier) likewise to business thinking. The neurologist who coined the term and convinced President Nixon to promote it "saw the HMO as a business model that could bring the methods of the industrial revolution to health care: 'conversion to larger units of production, technological innovation, division of labor, substitution of capital for labor, vigorous competition, and profitability as the mandatory condition of survival.'"

their patients' scans themselves, so that the insurance payments go to them rather than the hospital. They figure out ways to increase their high-margin work and decrease their low-margin work. This is a business, after all. In a few cases [a] hospital executive told me he'd seen the behavior cross over into what seemed like outright fraud. "I've had doctors here come up to me and say, 'You want me to admit patients to your hospital, you're going to have to pay me.'" [One cardiac surgeon commented that] "Medicine has become a pig trough here. . . . We took a wrong turn when doctors stopped being doctors and became businessmen." (pp. 12, 17)

I am not my doctors' "customer," thank you; these people are professionals with whom I trust my health. I don't give some hospital my "business," because I am not a buyer who wishes to beware. Nor do I "consume" health care services, because they might consume me. I hope that my physicians and nurses are not "human resources" who need to be "empowered," but rather dedicated human beings who are personally engaged. Diseases are not "markets," and professional health care services are not "products" to be plucked off some shelf at arm's length.

I suspect that, like most people, I no more want my hospital to act like a stock market corporation than I want it to act like a government bureaucracy. (How to reconcile this comes in the next myth.) **Keep out the dogmatic technocrats of both business and government, thank you, and replace them with thoughtful analysts.**

WHEN *BEING* A BUSINESS IS BAD FOR OUR HEALTH CARE

Businesses can logically provide many health care supplies and equipment as well as certain services such as laboratory tests.

But beyond that we had better be careful. "'Consumer-based' medicine has been a bust everywhere it has been tried" (Krugman, 2011).[2] Moreover,

> a free market only works when the consumer can use buying power to influence the price and quality of goods. In the current healthcare system, insurance is usually purchased by third parties (i.e., employers), not by the consumer directly. Also, healthcare is not a discretionary desire. As a result, the consumer is not in charge of directing the market and thus there is no feedback loop to increase quality or reduce cost. The current system is not a free-market but is instead a for-profit system driven by private insurance providers who are immune to the checks and balances associated with the free-market ideal. This system, which has been in place for decades, has led to increases in healthcare expenditures, poorer health outcomes, and less choice in providers. (Sarpel et al., 2008: 4)

Add to this the fact that health care deals with decisions of life and death, which "often must be made under conditions in which the patient is incapacitated, under severe stress, or

---

[2] Herzlinger (p. 61) cited example after example of failed efforts to run aspects of health care in business, each time offering a different excuse. In one, it was because status quo physicians "resent[ed] direct-to-consumer advertising" (p. 4, which many non-physicians also consider aberrations that distort information). In another, it was because "community doctors bad-mouthed" the company's "quality of care," also because of "the lack of health services expertise of its major investor, a venture capitalist firm that typically bankrolled high-tech start-ups" (p. 5). At one point, Herzlinger did cite what she considered a success story, HCA (originally Hospital Corporation of America), a company that paid the U.S. government $1.7 billion, the largest fraud settlement in American history, for alleged overbilling the public Medicare and Medicaid programs. Herzlinger commented, rather astonishingly, "Some people wondered whether a nonprofit institution would have paid so dearly for its alleged misdeeds." In any event, "the company weathered the crisis and . . . has continued to perform well." One has to wonder whether Herzlinger meant this example to support or to undermine her case.

needs action immediately, with no time for discussion, let alone comparison shopping" (Krugman, 2011).

WHEN *ACTING* LIKE A BUSINESS IS HARDLY BETTER

Hospitals and other health care institutions can certainly learn from business, about "improved capital budgeting, financial monitoring, and accounting systems" in order to get "better value for health expenditures" (Marmor, 2007: 8). Every kind of institution can learn from what business does well, just as every kind of business can learn from what other kinds of institutions do well. But that does not mean they should be acting like businesses.

Pollock, in her book *NHS plc* (2004), described some effects of the adoption of business practices on the National Health Service of England. For example, as a consequence of the purchaser/provider change, the NHS was inundated with management consultants, auditors, and lawyers "responsible for drawing up hundreds of thousands of contracts." She described the NHS as using a "supermarket model of care," thanks to advisors who were actually CEOs of supermarkets and banks (pp. 224, 226). Perhaps most indicative of the infiltration of business mentality in the NHS has been its ubiquitous use of the term "CEO." People all over the place strut around under this label, talking about "my hospital," etc., as if they own the place.

Not-for-profit hospitals, particularly in the United States, have hardly been immune to this onslaught of business thinking. Here are some comments from the heads of five such hospitals who attended a workshop with NHS people (in Best, 2007):

- [Our hospital's] market research department actively solicits patient and community views, feeding these through to our forecasting and marketing teams. We are also very strong on competitor analysis (p. 6).

- Some of our services lose money if assessed in isolation ... but we have about 50 physicians in small communities who make lots of referrals in high margin specialties (p. 6).
- All five ... at the workshop [claimed to] invest heavily in marketing their services—market surveys, focus groups, patient follow-up surveys, advertising and so on. What was marketed, however, was perhaps surprising [not so much of clinical quality as the "patient experience" and the reputation of the hospital] (p. 6).
- One CEO states that "We market directly to potential patients on amenities, services, facilities, concierge, private waiting rooms, free Starbuck's coffee and salt water aquariums in the emergency room." All five ... also invest heavily in "image" and "branding" (p. 6).
- The five U.S. CEOs were unanimous in their view that to compete successfully, their organizations needed to grow. This encompasses both growth in revenues as well as market share. The reasons for this include ... reducing unit costs [and being able to invest] in the latest technology [etc., but also to] maintain their "bond rating" ... which requires ... a minimum of 2 to 3 percent return on investment (p. 7).

Consider the effects of all of this on the costs of health care in the United States.

Best did report that the CEOs "felt genuinely accountable to their communities," including the provision of what they called "unprofitable services." As one put it, "If everything we did had to be profitable, there wouldn't be any point in being in our business" (p. 13). Still a business!

HEALTH CARE AS A CALLING

Can anyone possibly believe that most physicians, nurses, and other health care professionals work as hard and conscientiously as they do, in the face of so much pressure, tragedy, and frustration, in order to maximize "value" on some real or pretend line? Many of them, including some of the best, work on fixed salary, are beholden to no shareholders, and receive no bonuses for their performance. These people are not donkeys, looking forward to some carrot.

Far more important is their sense of accomplishment as well as the acclaim of their peers. As Abe Fuks put it, there exists "a latent drive in the people of health care to do the right thing." Shall we put them into corporate-type hierarchies with financial incentives to make them more efficient? What a perfect way to destroy their effectiveness. (Consider the demise of effective research, as discussed earlier, in some of the large pharmaceutical companies.)

The field of health care may be appropriately supplied by businesses, but in the delivery of its most basic services, it is not a business at all, nor should it be run like one. At its best, it is a calling. Where else are people more inclined to serve, in the noblest sense of the term? Sure, doctors like to make money. Don't we all? But there can be easier ways for smart people to do that. And the nurses, usually at least as dedicated, don't even get to earn that kind of money. As for the managers, often in the trickiest of jobs, especially in hospitals that are so difficult to manage, it is dedication to health care as a calling that keeps many of them going conscientiously.

Sholom Glouberman wrote in response to an early draft of the above that "altruism has been one of the casualties of the growing dysfunction in health care," with "reduced institutional loyalty" that has perhaps discouraged "the brightest young people with strong altruistic motivation" from "pursuing careers in the health field" (personal correspondence, 2008). But happily there are exceptions, as noted in the accompanying box.

Medicine Motivated

In his article cited earlier, Atul Gawande (2009a) quoted a surgeon who claimed that the practice of medicine "has changed completely. Before, it was about how to do a good job. Now it is about 'How much will you benefit?'" Gawande contrasted this with what he found in the Mayo Clinic, which can help to explain its reputation:

> The Mayo Clinic . . . is among the highest-quality, lowest-cost health-care systems in the country. A couple of years ago, I spent several days there as a visiting surgeon. Among the things that stand out from that visit was how much time the doctors spent with patients. There was no churn—no shuttling patients in and out of rooms while the doctor bounces from one to another. . . . One patient had colon cancer and a number of other complex issues, including heart disease. The physician spent an hour with her, sorting things out. He phoned a cardiologist with a question.

> "I'll be there," the cardiologist said.

> Fifteen minutes later, he was. They mulled over everything together . . . cleared the patient for surgery, and the operating room gave her a slot the next day. The whole interaction was astonishing to me. . . .

> The core tenet of the Mayo Clinic is: "The needs of the patient come first"—not the convenience of the doctors, not their revenues. The doctors and nurses, and even the janitors, sat in meetings almost weekly, working on ideas to make the service and the care better, not to get more money out of patients. . . . But decades ago Mayo recognized that the first thing it needed to do was eliminate the

financial barriers. It pooled all the money the doctors and the hospital system received and began paying everyone a salary, so that the doctors' goal in patient care couldn't be increasing their income . . . almost by happenstance, the result has been lower costs." (14–15)

Gawande's conclusion:

"You come to realize that we are witnessing a battle for the soul of American medicine. Somewhere in the United States at this moment, a patient with chest pain, or a tumor, or a cough is seeing a doctor. And the damning question we have to ask is whether the doctor is set up to meet the needs of the patient, first and foremost, or to maximize revenue." (p. 16)

SUMMING UP THE FIXES

To conclude this discussion about mergers, markets, measurements, leadership, administrative engineering, being business-like if not actually a business, and the rest of these easy solutions, **it is time to recognize that the greatest failure in health care may be these very fixes themselves.**

Health care . . . ranks high on every dimension for the conventional wisdom about how transformation occurs. Strong leadership, noble vision, clear outcomes, predictable and regulated practices, tight measures, high influence expertise, major investment in training. So, how is it going? Not great. (Block, 2008: 171)[3]

---

[3] Or as Denis described it: "Bureaucratic or political reform projects that seek to introduce rapid change to the entire health care system result in major upheavals, without necessarily effecting any in-depth change in practices and procedures" (2002: 3).

There has been great pressure to cut costs, largely as a consequence of advances in expensive treatments combined with our unwillingness to pay for them. Because many clinical professionals have been reluctant to address the costs they help to incur, or at least to cooperate with other people who are trying to do that, these other people—analysts, economists, accountants, administrative engineers, managers, etc.—have stepped into the breech. Many have worked diligently to keep the lid on the escalating costs, and they have often succeeded, sometimes too well: with consequent deterioration in the quality of services.

There is the need to proceed differently in facing the escalating costs of health care: with scalpels instead of axes, out of the administrative offices and into the operating rooms, of all kinds. What looks good on paper can wreak havoc in practice because administrative prescriptions are often simple whereas the reality of where they have to work is often complex. **Simple detached solutions rarely resolve the intricate problems of health care. Instead, ways need to be found to combine the efforts of dedicated administrators with devoted professionals.** We will return to this after discussing our last two myths.

— 8 —

Myths #8 and #9

Overall, health care is rightly left to the private sector, for the sake of efficiency and choice. Overall, health care is rightly controlled by the public sector, for the sake of equality and economy.

You are most likely suffering from one of these imperatives, depending on where you live. In fact, **if you live where the services are largely private, you hear much about the role of the public sector, while if you live where the services are mostly public, you hear much about the role of the private sector. That is because nowhere in the world today can the field of health care function without the serious involvement of both government controls and market forces. The issue is not which, but how much of each, and where.**

But for many of the key services, accept neither. Efficiency, choice, equality, and economy certainly matter. But quality matters, too, and so does the personal engagement of providers and users alike. We have already discussed how efficiency and economy can reduce quality, and how choice can be dubious when information favors the provider. Moreover, equality (including accessibility) can reduce the quality of service to some lowest common denominator. As noted earlier, **at its essence, the management of health care has to face the reconciliation of quantity, quality, and equality.**

What we often fail to recognize is that there are three sectors in society, not two: the public, the private, and alongside them, the *plural*. Key to quality and engagement may be this other one, as we shall soon discuss.

THE GREAT DIVIDE?

The extent to which dogma dominates the great debate over public versus private health care is astonishing, even among reputable scholars,

Porter and Teisberg didn't address the role of government in health care; they dismissed it. "Government-imposed regulations . . . are never a real solution" (2006: 382), they claimed, ignoring much of the world where they are.[1] And here is the opening of their 2004 article: "The U.S. health care system has registered unsatisfactory performance in both cost and quality over many years. While this may be expected in a state-controlled sector, it is nearly unimaginable in a competitive market" (p. 21). Really?

---

[1] Including Canada, which as noted earlier has lower costs and better results. Where Porter and Teisberg do refer to other countries, their bias often remains. "In the French health care system, for example, patients have the choice of private care. Private clinics account for over 40 percent of health care delivery by volume but only 22 percent of the costs, highlighting the efficiency advantage of the private sector" (2006: 377). Only in an accompanying footnote do they acknowledge that public hospitals do more research than private ones, "so the difference is not all due to efficiency" (p. 443). Moreover, no mention is made that the French are inclined to favor public hospitals for their serious medical problems, which are obviously costlier.

This is quite the claim in an article about the importance of using factual data to make decisions about health care.[2] Surprisingly, these authors say nothing in this regard about the Veterans Administration, the "largest integrated healthcare system in the United States." It is public sector, has been highly regarded, and considered to be cost-effective (see Longman, 2012; the Veterans Administration does get three brief mentions elsewhere in the Porter and Teisberg book [pp. 110, 131, and 438], two of them complimentary).

But is this great divide so great as it seems?

Consider Canada and the U.S. They sit on the two sides of this divide. As noted earlier, they also sit on two sides of what has been called the longest unguarded border in the world—except when it comes to health care.

On the north side, Canada has what is considered to be one of the most socialized health services in the world: everyone is covered for all basic medical and hospital services, out of general tax revenues. We Canadians call it Medicare and guard it with a vengeance, gleefully telling each other horror stories about private health care in the United States. Medicare is not just a cherished program for many Canadians, but a sacred pillar of our democracy.[3]

---

[2] More telling still is this comment from their book: "Government-run health systems in other parts of the world are encountering increasing problems with quality, costs, and rationalizing" (2006: 324). True enough. But in comparison with private sector health care in the United States?

[3] In 2004, the Canadian Broadcasting Corporation held a contest to vote for "the greatest Canadian." And the winner: Tommy Douglas. If you are not Canadian, don't worry that you never heard of Tommy Douglas: his highest position was premier of the small province of Saskatchewan (population less than a million at the time), followed by the leadership of the small social democratic party at the federal level. Tommy Douglas won the vote because he brought Medicare to his province in 1962 and was subsequently instrumental in pushing a minority Liberal government to do the same thing for the whole country, beginning in 1971.

On the south side of this border, the United States has one of the most private health care services in the world. Many Americans are covered by their personal insurance or that of their employer, but many others have had no coverage at all. So-called Obamacare may have changed this somewhat, but the basics of American health care have not changed. Some Americans, too, take great glee in telling each other horror stories about Canadian health care (at least when they are not telling each other horror stories about their own health care).

Now for a reality check. About 30 percent of Canadian health care is not funded by government (dental services and pharmaceuticals outside of hospitals for most of the population, etc.), while almost two-thirds of American health care *is* funded by government (Medicare for the elderly, Medicaid, the Veterans Administration, etc.[4] [AJPH, 2016], also including public employees' private health insurance coverage and tax subsidies to health care).

BEYOND CRUDE AND CRASS

This great divide is narrow in one other significant respect: for many of health care's more professional services, it is neither the public nor the private sector that performs best. They can, of course, do well, such as the public Veterans Administration just mentioned and some private hospitals in India and Japan. (In France, quite a different place from the U.S. and Canada with regard

---

[4] Many of the other developed countries fall somewhere between what the OECD has called Canada's "national health service model" and America's "private insurance model" (Litvak, 2008: 5) with what are called mixed models. Some subscribe to a "social insurance model" that divides costs among employers and employees, dispensed through non-profit insurance funds. Okma et al., in a 2010 study of health reform in Chile, Israel, Singapore, Switzerland, Taiwan, and the Netherlands, concluded that "no country has fully privatized or fully nationalized its entire health care system."

to government the public hospitals seem to do rather well.) But frequently **government controls are too crude and market forces too crass for many professional health care services.** Who wants to choose between crude and crass when it comes to our health?[5]

So if not the public or private sectors, then what? The answer is easy, in fact all around us. We are so used to being on one or other side of the left-right political spectrum that we fail to recognize a sector that need not be left nor right. I prefer to call it the *plural sector,* although you may know it by another in a long string of inadequate labels, such as the third sector (as if it is third-rate, an afterthought), the home of not-for-profits or of NGOs (even though governments are not-for-profit and businesses are nongovernmental), or civil society (a term that often confuses—compared with uncivil society?). Calling it the plural sector signifies the sector's variety of institutions and their varied forms of ownership as well as the need to find a label for this sector to help it take its rightful place alongside those called public and private. (These ideas and those that follow are drawn from my book *Rebalancing Society: Radical Renewal Beyond Left, Right, and Center* [2015].)

WELCOME TO THE PLURAL SECTOR, FOR THE SAKE OF QUALITY AND ENGAGEMENT

The vast majority of hospitals on both sides of that guarded health care border between Canada and the United States are neither private nor public. In other words, they are not the property of governments or of private investors. In America, that

---

[5] Consider this comment by the executive director of the Nevada State Medical Association, who had been a vehement opponent of earlier government reforms proposed by Hillary Clinton: "I was the pit dog for the attack out here. It was too easy. But I never imagined that the government would implode and leave the field to the insurance industry and the corporations that got in the first floor. What we have today is market medicine" (Hitchens, 1998: 57).

includes about 70 percent of all hospitals (called "voluntary"), among them the most respected. And in Canada, that figure has been close to 100 percent (Taylor, 2002: 1418).

Canadian hospitals may be mostly funded by government but they are not owned by them: historically they have had their own boards of directors, donors, and volunteers. (See the follow-up box below on "Coup d'état in Quebec." England, by the way, has been moving in the opposite direction, turning many of its public hospitals and other community services into "foundation trusts." Discussed further in the box below, it is remarkable how often in health care different regimes change in contradictory directions, in ignorance of each other's experiences.)

Coup d'état in Quebec

In combining the 200 health care institutions (hospitals, community care clinics, etc.), into 28 agglomerations (called CISSSs), as discussed earlier, the government of Quebec not only reduced the managers (directors general) by that number, but also the boards of directors. There is now one for each agglomeration, a majority of whose members are appointed by the minister of health, as are the 28 president-directors general. This one person now controls all of this. And the reporting line for each agglomeration now goes straight to this minister. Where many of these institutions were founded by community groups or religious orders and have been deeply embedded locally as independent trusts, now they are, in effect, government agencies. In a newspaper article, Lysianne Gagnon (2014) called this "an abuse of power," for a "system already too centralized," which has ended up as an "autocracy."

In effect, the government of Quebec has nationalized all the plural sector health care institutions of Quebec, hospitals included. It is as if the plural sector no longer exists in Quebec health care. This coup is probably illegal—many of these institutions have charters and long histories—but which one is going to challenge the government that provides most of its funding?

The Quebec government claims that these reforms will put "the patient at the center of decision-making," improve "circulation of clinical information," and "reduce bureaucracy." Words are cheap. And community, as well as the plural sector, are irrelevant, in the view of this government.

So welcome to the overlooked plural sector, for the sake of quality and engagement. A century of obsessive disputes between left and right, governments and markets, nationalizations and privatizations, Smith and Marx, etc., has blinded us to the enormous amount of activity, and benefits, that lie beyond these pairs.

PLURAL OWNERSHIP AND THE COMMONS

Some of the organizations of this sector—for example, cooperatives—are owned by their members, but without the right to sell their one share to other members. (The United States, by the way, has more co-op memberships than people.) Others are owned by no one. Examples include those trusts and voluntary hospitals mentioned earlier, as well as the Red Cross, Doctors Without Borders, and the laboratories that brought us penicillin, insulin, and Salk vaccine.[6]

---

[6] I might add that group medical practices, while technically in the private sector, have characteristics similar to member-owned cooperatives in the plural sector. They share facilities but usually not revenues. (There is a vast difference between a few physicians sharing a space and a giant chain of clinics listed on a stock exchange.) On the other hand, as Gawande described the Mayo Clinic, quoted earlier, with the doctors pooling their revenues, this non-owned organization also has characteristics of member-ownership. Brazil does have cooperative hospitals that are member-owned by the physicians, while Japan has cooperative ones that are owned by the potential users (not just the actual patients).

If no one owns these institutions, then in a sense everybody owns them. But don't confuse this kind of ownership with that found in the private sector, or even in the public sector. It's a form of property called the *commons*: owned implicitly by the members of a community who share the benefits (as we might say about our community hospitals). Common property used to be prominent, then got pushed aside, and is now making a comeback. In health care, the commons may prove to be especially significant, as discussed in the accompanying box and elaborated upon later.

The Crucial Commons in Health Care

We think of property as private. Even "public property" is in a sense private: owned not by you and me so much as by our governments, albeit on our behalf.

Common Property is held by people "jointly and together rather than separately and apart" (Rowe, 2008: 2). The air we breathe can be called common property, and so too is the water for irrigation shared by farmers in various parts of the world. Indeed, the Boston Common, now a park, was once the place where the landless people of that city could graze their cows.

But the commons has had a rough ride since those days in Boston. In 1968, a geographer named Garrett Hardin published an article entitled "The Tragedy of the Commons," about why such property did not work. He later modified his position (Rowe, 2008), but not before the article created a tragedy of its own: economists used it to dismiss the very idea.

The commons is now coming back, in interesting ways. Think of open source systems such as Wikipedia, freely available to all of us, as authors as well as readers. No fees. "Today this [common property] model is reappearing in many precincts of the economy at large—from the revival of traditional main streets, public spaces, and community gardens to the resistance to the corporate enclosure of university research and the genetic substrate of material life" (Rowe: 2008: 139).

To extend the example of Wikipedia directly into one of health care's key issues: "The greatest benefits of open-source health IT come from the opportunities that are created when different hospitals, clinics, individual doctors, and researchers are able to share records and stores of data with each other," compared with those data being locked away by separate institutions. How can doctors "switch IT providers if they can't extract patient data, or if they must pay a monopolist's price to do so. In the software industry, this is known as 'vendor capture'" (Longman, 2012: 116–117).

Most broadly, who owns our health? Certainly not any government or insurance company, not even just ourselves, because some of our illnesses are common: we share them through viruses, and thus experience epidemics. (The Japanese understand this well, since when they have a cold or the flu, in the spirit of community they wear masks to protect others, not themselves.) Our health as common property can also be seen where people cooperate to ensure a safe environment.

Well, then, who should own the treatments for our diseases? Many medical discoveries become common property, to be used by colleagues around the world for everyone's benefit. Jonas Salk liked this model so well that he refused to patent his discovery, with this comment: "Who owns my polio vaccine? The people. Could you patent the sun?" (Stay tuned: some pharmaceutical company is bound to try.[7])

Pharmaceutical advances are hardly made in a vacuum: many were made possible by basic research, sponsored by

---

[7] One company has managed to patent a couple of our genes, with the consequence that it has been able to charge more than $3,000 for a breast cancer test (Pollack, 2011).

governments and carried out in not-for-profit laboratories. (There have, in fact, been battles over what the companies should be paying for these contributions to their research.) Moreover, as noted earlier, this pricing is made possible by patents that are state-granted monopolies. How can any government allow companies to charge "what the market will bear" for life-and-death products? Does the collapse of decency in our societies know no bounds?

Communism taught us that a society with hardly any private property cannot function effectively. Capitalism is teaching us that a society with hardly anything but private property is not much better. **Recognition of common property could be making a major difference in the effectiveness of health care—on the side of costs as well as benefits.**

PLURAL, PUBLIC, OR PRIVATE?

The following words appeared in *Becker's Hospital Review* (Page, 2011):

> [Private equity] funds are developing a strong interest in the healthcare sector. . . . A Pepperdine University poll at the end of last year found that 11 percent of private equity executives polled said they planned to invest in healthcare, up from 4.8 percent in summer 2010. "There will be aggregation of existing hospital companies, diversification into outpatient sectors, and more jostling among companies to pick up larger positions in local markets," . . . a general partner with [a] private equity firm told the *Wall Street Journal* last year.

Will this be good for health care? The evidence that compares for-profit with not-for-profit health care institutions—mainly, but not only, concerning hospitals—seems clear, and in the opinion of some who have studied it, "overwhelming":

While enthusiasts argue that for-profit facilities can provide medical services more efficiently and with a lower price tag, the vast majority of studies show the exact opposite. Research demonstrates that waiting lists and costs aren't reduced with private for-profit contracts—and American literature indicates that patients who receive care in for-profit facilities are more likely to die than those in non-profit ones. . . .

For example, a recent review of 149 studies and 20 years' worth of data looked at how these facilities performed against each other in the areas of access, quality, and cost-effectiveness. The researchers considered six types of institutions—hospitals, nursing homes, HMOs, hospices, dialysis centers, and psychiatric hospitals. They found that 88 of the studies concluded that non-profit centres performed better, while 43 studies found that the performance was no different. Only 18 studies found for-profit centres were better. The differences are particularly clear at psychiatric inpatient hospitals, where out of 17 studies, only one found for-profit facilities to be better (Canadian Health Services Research Foundation, 2004).[8]

---

[8] Moreover, "researchers found health spending was higher and increased faster in communities served by for-profit hospitals, compared to non-profit communities" (Canadian Health Services Research Foundation, 2004). "In 1999, Himmelstein and Woolhandler compared the cost of for-profit and not-for-profit hospitals in the United States—the latter includes all public, charitable, and veterans' hospitals. Of the two groups, it was the for-profits that led in such cost-cutting measures as the avoidance of charity care, the shortening of patients' hospital stays, the reduction of medical staffing levels, and the carrying out of detailed 'utilization reviews' of the hospitals' dealings with physicians and MCOs. But administrators were needed for all these tasks, and once these costs of administration were added to the for-profit hospitals' higher spending on consultants, marketing and advertising, the for-profit hospitals were between 3 and 11 percent *more* expensive than their not-for-profit counterparts" (Head, 2003: 139).

So, at the very least, **it is time to end claims about the superiority of private sector health care services over public sector ones, or vice versa. In important respects, plural sector services trump both.**

ENGAGEMENT AND COMMUNITYSHIP IN THE PLURAL SECTOR

Why should this be? Can the simple fact of ownership, by members or no one, be that significant? The short answer is yes; the long one is potentially so even if not always so.

External control of an organization, whether by private owners or public authorities, tends to centralize and formalize, namely bureaucratize, its structure (Mintzberg, 1979: 288–291; see also 1983: 146–147). That is partly because administrators are forced to spend more time looking up, and out, which widens the gap between themselves and the operations. As a consequence, they may rely more extensively on conventional hierarchy, and thus make greater use of performance measures and administrative engineering, all of which can weaken the professionals' natural engagement with their work—their sense of calling.

And how about community, the heart and soul of the plural sector and the home of so many of its organizations? *Indigenous* is defined in my Oxford dictionary as "originating or naturally occurring in a place." Much health care occurs naturally in a place, namely an identifiable geographic community. As noted earlier, there is certainly a role for specialized regional or national hospitals. But for the most part, health care services in hospitals and out tend to be not only located in the communities where they are delivered, but also deeply embedded in those communities. Indeed, the managers and professionals are often prominent members of these communities.

Years ago, in a famous article in sociology, Gouldner (1957) distinguished "cosmopolitans" from "locals." Health care is delivered mostly by locals, even if some are internationally renowned. Analysts and economists in health care who help to diffuse innovations from one community to others may more often be cosmopolitans, but they have no business seeking to detach many health care services from their local roots. To repeat, **community matters in health care, even if it is largely ignored in economics.**

Moreover, the most effective health care institutions themselves tend to function *as* communities in their own right. What I have called *communityship* (Mintzberg, 2006, 2009) describes a deep sense of engagement—commitment and loyalty—on the part of people associated with an organization, including professionals and other employees, managers, and even users of the services as well as volunteers. All can get quite attached to *their* institution, especially when it functions in the plural sector, rather than being the agency of some government or the division of some business. As one local put it when an earlier effort by the Quebec government sought to stack hospital boards with more of its own appointees, "Who would volunteer in a government hospital?" Or a private one for that matter?

Being part of a robust community, in contrast to working for a focused factory, helps to foster collaboration, which can enrich the quality of service. You might be a civil servant reporting to some detached government authority, or a human resource expected to maximize "value" for some shareholders you never met. Compare these with being engaged in a community whose colleagues see their work as a calling. As Gawande noted about a number of respected health services in the U.S., including Kaiser Permanente and Intermountain HealthCare: "All are not-for-profit institutions. And all have produced enviably higher quality and lower costs than the average American town enjoys" (2009a). Likewise, Mitchell et al. (2004) found that a large majority of Americans prefer plural sector nursing homes to private sector ones.

So **it is time to get past the great debate between government controls and market forces in health care, to recognize that for some of its most important services, both are inclined to weaken the role of local communities as well as that of communityship within the institutions, to the detriment of quality.**

DISENGAGEMENT IN THE PLURAL SECTOR

Allowed to be what they most naturally are, plural sector organizations tend to exhibit these characteristics of engagement and communityship. Unfortunately, too many are not so allowed. We all know about not-for-profit hospitals that have let people die while checking out their health insurance, and not-for-profit nursing homes that have mistreated the elderly. Sometimes this happens because these organizations have grown too large (communityship depends on personalized relationships) or because their funders, directors, or managers have forced them to act like businesses. But others have simply lost their way by failing to take advantage of functioning in the plural sector.

Moreover, the stronger the *engagement within* an institution and community, the greater the risk of *disengagement from* other institutions and communities. If public sector organizations can be crude and private sector organizations crass, then plural sector organizations can be closed. Think of those institutions whose fierce sense of pride has impeded collaboration with others. Think too of the many professional associations that have closed in on themselves. **We no more need closed professional control of health care than we need crude state control or crass market control.** This book pleads for greater devolution of influence toward the operations on the ground. But that will work only to the extent that professionals are prepared to collaborate, within and beyond their own specialties. To repeat, this field needs more collaboration, not more competition.

So the appropriate conclusion for Myths #8 and #9 is that no sector has any claim of being able to solve all the problems of health care, although greater recognition of the plural sector, so long overlooked, can certainly help. As we shall discuss in Part III, there are key roles for governments, businesses, and community institutions in health care.

To sum up Part I, **"If we always do as we always did, we will always get what we always got." In health care, we keep getting some excellent but mostly disjointed services, biased toward the treatment of acute diseases. Too often the quality of these services are distracted by administrative interventions, some of which may be necessary to keep the lid on costs, including their own.** We need to think differently about the management of health care, which is the subject of Part III. But first. . . .

PART II:
ORGANIZING

LET'S STOP HERE, between the myths of health care (Part I) and suggestions for the reframing of it (Part III), to take a good look at how health care is organized.

Human organization is essentially about *differentiation* and *integration* (Lawrence and Lorsch, 1967): breaking some overall mission into activities that can be carried out by individuals or teams—called the "division of labor"—and then putting these back together for a consolidated result.

But in between comes the problem. **Differentiation gets reified: *separations* arise that make it difficult to integrate activities.** And health care is one of those fields that suffers especially from this. It is wonderful at taking things apart—consider all those medical sub-subspecialties—but too often dreadful at putting them back together.

So before considering how the management of health care might be reframed, we need to understand in some detail how it differentiates, separates, and can better integrate its activities. We begin by describing three dimensions of differentiation: the specialized players of health care, the quadrants in which they play, and their playing practices. Then we consider three kinds of disruptive separations: curtains across the specialties, sheets over the patients, and walls and floors between the administrators. Finally, we consider two aspects of integration: the coordinating mechanisms that can be used, misused, or often not used, to integrate differentiated activities, and various forms of organizing that can encourage and impede integration in health care.

9

Differentiating

Widely understood, perhaps too much so, are the differentiations among the specialized *players* of health care. Less understood than they should be are the *quadrants* that separate care, cure, control, and community from each other. And perhaps in need of greater clarification are the *practices* that differentiate this fragmented field. Each is discussed in turn.

THE SPECIALIZED PLAYERS OF HEALTH CARE

These are the main players in health care:

a. First and foremost are you and me, individually and collectively, as *users*. Each of us alone and all of us together can make a great deal of difference, for better and for worse: by what we eat, how we influence our surroundings, whether or not we seek help, and how we use that help as well as go beyond it. We are usually called "patients" in this "system," but our roles as users go well beyond that.

b. Serving the users are the *providers*, all those people and institutions that deliver the operating services to us: in community health, public health, hospitals, and so on, via nursing, medicine, and other recognized operating professions as well as so-called alternate practices. Please note that all of these providers are themselves users, just as all the users are providers (every time we take an aspirin or bandage the knee of our child).

c. Reinforcing what the providers do are the *supporters* of the health care services, those people and institutions that aid the delivery of the providers: manufacturers of medicines, materials and instruments, volunteers, researchers, donors, and so on.

d. Next come the *administrative engineers*: systems analysts, accountants, economists, so on. Within hospitals, government ministries, insurance companies, etc., they develop and apply administrative programs, techniques, tools, and structures, many of these to control costs.

e. Finally, seeking to hold all this together are the *administrators* of health care, from the chiefs of medical practices and head nurses of the hospital wards through the managers of the hospitals and community service agencies, etc., to the central administrators in the insurance companies and the government ministries. (See also Kushlick, 1975.)

To state the sometimes overlooked obvious, **all the services delivered in this field—whether concerning health promotion, disease prevention, or the treatment of disease—focus on the interplay of the first and second groups: the users and the providers of the basic services.** The other three groups support this interplay. Health care, in other words, happens on the ground, where a physician writes a prescription and a nurse injects a vaccine, where a polluting pipe is sealed and a public service advertisement encourages people to exercise. Managers, economists, accountants, etc., may help to make these things happen, but they no more maintain anyone's health than does the admitting staff of a hospital or professors who write books about managing health care.

THE QUADRANTS OF HEALTH CARE

You may think, or at least hope, that these players play the same game. Not always, even if sometimes on the same turf. Imagine several people running down a field, one carrying a football, another kicking a soccer ball, a third bouncing a basketball. Suddenly the soccer player kicks the ball to the basketball player, calling out, "Urgent: We have a cardiac arrest in ophthalmology!"

These players play in different *quadrants*. Visualize the general hospital, as shown in the form of a Swiss cross in Figure 2 (from Glouberman and Mintzberg, 2001a, 2001b). This depicts **management as happening *down* (into the operations) or else *up* (out of them), also *in* (within the formal organization) or *out* (beyond its formal authority, even if inside its walls). The result is four basic quadrants of activity, which amount to four quite different worlds of the hospital, labeled cure, care, control, and community.**

Physicians, representing *cure*, are down and out (even if hardly as in the expression "down and out"): inside the operations but usually outside its formal hierarchy of authority. Mostly, historically at least, they work *in* the hospital but not *for* the hospital. Nurses, representing *care*, are down and in: inside the operations and subject to the formal authority of the hospital. General managers, representing *control* (especially fiscal control, as well as control of everyone but the physicians), are up and in: removed from the clinical operations but forming the essence of the administrative hierarchy. And board members as well as volunteers, among others, are up and out, representing *community*: they connect directly neither to the operations nor

FIGURE 2 **Quadrants in Health Care:**
Four Worlds in the Acute Institution

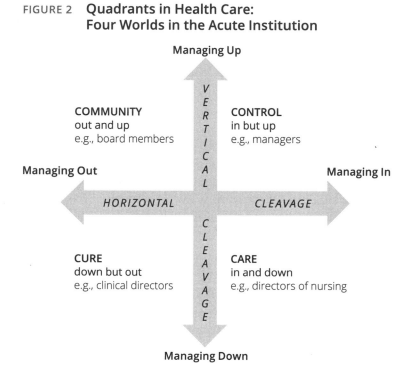

to the administrative hierarchy. (At a meeting I once attended of an advisory committee of a hospital board, these two worlds were perfectly illustrated by dark suits around one end of the table and white coats around the other.)

Sholom and I proposed a metaphor for each of these quadrants. In the quadrant of cure, the physicians use the *scalpel*, deftly, to slice out not only tumors in the body but also pieces of the budget (e.g., for equipment). The general managers, together with their administrative engineers, have to rely on the *ax*, to hack out savings in those budgets. As for community, the board members of the hospital depend on the *gavel*, to hit the managers over the head as well as to make loud noises at their meetings. As for the nurses, in the quadrant of care, the metaphor is the *scissors*, which they use to cut up cotton wool to place over all these wounds—physiological, psychological, and organizational.

"For the last hundred years the general hospital has been the key battleground for the various forces arrayed in the division of labor in health care. There seems no reason why this should change now" (in *An Introduction to the Social History of Nursing*, by Dingwall et al., 1988). If you work in some other institution of health care, say a community clinic or public health, I imagine that you can picture the four quadrants there as well, although perhaps not as sharply as in the hospital.

Then Sholom and I drew another Swiss cross, to represent health care overall (Figure 3). We put the hospital itself—the whole of the previous figure—in the lower-left quadrant, representing *acute cure—down into* the delivery of service, but *out* in the sense of being difficult to control directly. Next to it,

FIGURE 3 **Four Worlds in Society at Large**

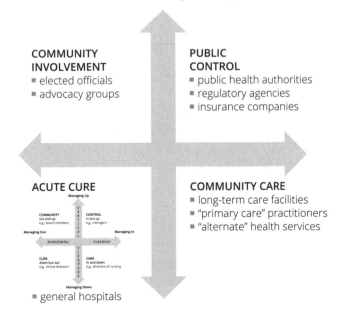

down but *in*, we put *community care*, in the form of primary care, public health, long-term facilities, etc. *Up* and *in*, on the top right, we located *institutional control*, whether by insurance companies or government health authorities, etc., as well as the professional associations that control certain behaviors of their members. Finally, *up* and *out*, on the top left, we placed *community involvement* of all kinds, including advocacy groups (e.g., for patient rights) and various health associations.

THE PRACTICES OF HEALTH CARE

Figure 4 presents a map of wellness and illness that I developed to display in one place the range of practices used in the care of health and the treatment of disease. Seeing all this together— on one diagram—can be a first step toward a more systemic perspective.

The upper portion of the map shows you and I, in the middle, as not only mind and body, but also spirit and type (e.g., how we respond to various treatments). To our left are various sources of wellness (sanitation, lifestyle, nutrition), and to our right, various dimensions of illness (mild to critical, chronic and acute) as well as the various purposes of the interventions (to heal, cure, care, rehabilitate, stabilize, and palliate).

The lower portion of the map is a table that plots the major forms of intervention, on two dimensions. Shown horizontally across the top is a continuum from the promotion of health through the prevention of disease to its treatment. And listed vertically down the rows are four basic ways to intervene, labeled *mediation* (communicating, as in psychotherapy and educating); *manipulation* (touching or otherwise influencing the body physically, as in exercise and chiropractic); *ingestion* (swallowing or some other form of absorption into the body, as in diet and the taking of medicines, including homeopathy, a diluted form of ingestion); and *incursion* (cutting or otherwise

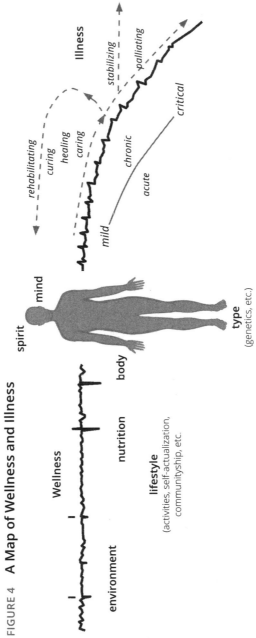

FIGURE 4 **A Map of Wellness and Illness**

123

FIGURE 4   **A Map of Wellness and Illness** *continued*

Forms of Intervention

	Promotion of Health	Prevention of Illness	Treatment of Disease
Mediation	Education Attitudes Relationships Affiliations	Meditation Hypnotism	Psychotherapy
Manipulation	Yoga Exercise Massage	Biofeedback	Physiotherapy Chiropractic/Osteopathy Energy Healing
Ingestion	Diet	Vitamins Homeopathy Eco-Recovery Herbal Medicines	Pharmaceuticals
Incursion		Innoculation Acupuncture	Dentistry Surgery

Note: Forms of intervention listed are meant to be suggestive, not comprehensive, and tentative. Their placement suggests their most common, but not exclusive, application.

penetrating the body, as in inoculation, surgery, and acupuncture, a shallow form of incursion). Not shown but evident are all the subpractices within these forms of intervention, such as in the different forms of surgery. Note that as we proceed down these rows, the distinction between cure and care sharpens: it is least evident in mediation, most evident in incursion.

Separating

Across these various groupings of differentiation can be found a variety of separations: of curtains across the practices, of sheets over the patients, and of walls and floors between the administrators.

CURTAINS ACROSS THE PRACTICES

Curtains are vertical barriers to horizontal collaboration. Too often, these are based on artificial status rather than functional needs. **Differentiation into specialized practices is necessary, but allowing artificial barriers to separate them is not: health care no more needs an overemphasis on status than business needs an overemphasis on authority.** Shown in Figure 5, laid over the operating quadrants of health care, are four of the most prominent of these curtains, labeled cure, acute, medical, and professional. Each is discussed in turn.

FIGURE 5 **The Curtains of Health Care**

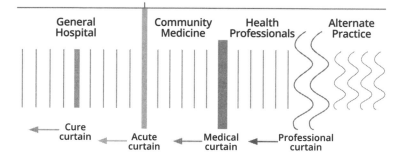

The Cure Curtain

Care and cure may make for nice, neat differentiation, but sometimes this distinction is too nice, too neat. It may work in surgery, but how about psychiatry, or geriatrics? There are several ways in which this distinction can break down:

First, care can help cure. We know that the courses of certain illnesses can be affected by the surroundings of the patient—a caring family, sympathetic treatment, attention to cleanliness. We often get better when we feel better.

Second, care can reduce the need for cure. Having a baby is not a disease. Yet unnecessary cesarean sections convert that experience into one. Moreover, sympathetic care offered by midwives can reduce the need for medical intervention. In a similar vein, the use of milder forms of treatment—for example, acupuncture and homeopathy—can sometimes reduce the need for more radical surgical or pharmaceutical treatments.

Third, care can preempt cure. We care for ourselves in order to reduce the need for cure. We care about what we eat and whether we do regular exercise. Likewise, we care for each other—for example, by showing concern for what those close to us eat and do. And by reducing waste, we care for the planet on which we live, and so improve health. All of this can be much more cost-effective than having to rely instead on subsequent cures. (It has been claimed that the greatest health advance of all time was cleaning up the water supply.)

Fourth, cure can be no more than care. How much of what we call cure is really just care? Consider all the medical interventions that are palliative—not only in geriatrics, but even in major surgeries that alleviate rather than reverse particular conditions.

What needs to be eliminated is not the distinction between care and cure so much as its misuse, especially when it works against the promotion of health and the prevention of disease. **In the world of "health care," care needs to be strengthened and brought into better balance with cure.**

The Acute Curtain

Between hospitals and the rest of health care is an *acute curtain,* to the left of which are treated the most serious diseases, often with the most expensive technologies. (There are, of course, other kinds of curtains within this, for example, between tertiary and other hospitals as well as between higher and lower status hospital physicians. **Physicians who like to belittle hierarchies of authority are often slaves to their own hierarchies of status.**) In fact, when many of us think about health care, we tend to focus on hospitals, even though they account for only about 30 percent of the total expenditures. Consider all the people with minor ailments who go to hospital emergency rooms, and all the management professors who write books about health care with too many examples from hospitals.

The Medical Curtain

To the right of the acute curtain is the *medical curtain,* which separates services provided by physicians in general practice and community institutions from the services of other professionals—psychologists, pharmacists, physiotherapists, and so on. Here again, what is a functional division of labor can reify into dysfunctional separations. My daughter Susie, who has worked with families of the mentally ill for many years, wrote me a pointed note after reading an early draft of this book:

> One of the things that struck me . . . is that, for the most part, you make reference to two groups of people: the managers and the physicians. . . . Although the [book] critiques top down decision making . . . I find it interesting, or rather, misleading, that you consider physicians to be the ones on the ground. You could take almost the exact same argument you are making, but replace the word great leader by physician and the word physician by social worker (or community worker or even possibly nurse). In health care, physicians are not on the bottom, they are on the top.
>
> In psychiatry, for example, they probably have the least contact with the patients but the most power . . . [making decisions] that are not in line with what the people on the ground are observing or thinking. . . . If you want to rethink the structure of health care, I think that you need to reconsider where the ground is. (Susie Mintzberg, in personal correspondence, 2010; see also Kushlick, 1975).

A Note on the Art and Craft of the "Science" of Medicine

With this medical curtain being perhaps the most impassable, a discussion about the cloth from which it is woven (and used increasingly by other health care professions)—namely, "science" and "evidence"—is in order here.

Being *scientific*—better still, having your work defined as a science—is very fashionable. Many fields lay claim to it, including medicine. But **medicine is not a science at all. Science is about** the search for truth; medicine is about treating the ill. (Of course, medical research is about the search for truth.) **Medicine is a practice. It certainly *uses* science, indeed a good deal of science, which is one of the things that make it a profession. But so, too, does it use experience—indeed, a good deal of that—to supplement the formal evidence, or proceed in its absence. And this makes medicine a *craft* as well.**

As noted earlier, physicians in our health management master's program report that experience is no less important in their own practices than is evidence. That is why the training in medical school, to learn the underlying sciences (anatomy, physiology, etc.), has to be followed by internship on the job, to gain experience before full practice can begin.

And the best of medical practice depends on creative insights, to adapt to the unexpected, which is what makes it an *art* as well. Consider this passage from a paper by Peter Vaill entitled "Managing as a Performing Art," except that I have replaced the word *manager* with *physician*.

> Science selects phenomena to study scientifically and seeks to standardize and regularize these phenomena; that is, control their variability. The [physician] on the other hand, is always confronted with mixes of phenomena.... The [physician] cannot choose to banish from the system elements for which there is no adequate science. (1989: 121)

But too often evidence is seen as motherhood, or at least truth, as is science. Who can possibly be against evidence? Me, for one. At least when the use of evidence becomes obsessive—a club to beat up on experience. Back we go to that rock called hard data, which is evidence: turn it over and have a look at what might be crawling underneath.

Lots of errors, for one thing. No one has invented the perfect research method. All are flawed, and that can lead to misguided conclusions. Consider how many widely accepted scientific

findings, such as in the use of mammograms or calcium sup-
plements, have been subsequently overturned.

As has been noted, science is about the search for truth.
But **the truth is never found. Good evidence may get us
closer, but never there.** If you doubt this, please read the
accompanying box.

Truth?

In 1492 Christopher Columbus discovered truth: that the world
is round, not flat. Did he really? Looking out my window, I
can assure you that the world is neither round nor flat. It
is bumpy: I see a mountain. That's evidence too. Moreover,
we now have evidence that the world bulges at the equator.
That's not round.

Theories are never true because they are simplifications of
reality—words and symbols on paper and screen, not reality
itself. What they can be is useful, in context. No one since
Columbus has ever corrected for the curvature of the Earth
when designing a football field in Holland. The flat Earth theory
has worked quite well for that, thank you. But everyone since
who has sailed a ship has had to rely on the round Earth theory
(albeit sometimes to reach an island, whose very existence
rebuts both theories).

So what are we to make of this? First, that we need to continue
our search for truth while recognizing that we shall never
attain it. And second, that theories should not be rejected
because they are false, only because they are not useful in a
particular context. Karl Popper (1934) wrote a famous book
about research as the falsifiability of theories. A secretary of
mine once misspelled his name as Propper.

In addition to the errors of evidence are the biases that can be buried inside evidence. People particularly enamored of evidence may be inclined to overlook these biases. Sure, evidence of a systematic nature can expose the biases of experience. (My favorite example of such a bias is a claim I once heard on the radio by a guy who ran a clinic for treating baldness: that he never met a bald man who was not obsessed with his baldness. No kidding!) But if you believe that systematic research does away with biases, then you have been ignoring an awful lot of systematic evidence to the contrary.

See, for example, Mitroff (1974), about the furious battles among eminent geologists over the rocks collected on the moon. Or in health care, see Freedman's (2010) article in *The Atlantic* on "Lies, Damned Lies, and Medical Science," which reviews evidence about evidence-based medicine. He refers to a well-known medical critic who was astonished by the errors he found to have been committed in research, concerning the questions asked, the patients recruited, the measurements taken, and the results presented.

We have already discussed the biases in favor of disease treatment over health promotion, and within the former, toward acute interventions. So, too, have we seen the biases in medicine that favor measurements and fancy technologies. Too often this has worked to the detriment of practices that cannot rely on such technologies, and against illnesses whose outcomes are less amenable to measurement (e.g., in psychiatric and autoimmune cases). As Gawande put it: "fragmented, disorganized, and inconsistent, the system is neglectful of low-profit services like mental-health care, geriatrics, and primary care, and almost giddy in its overuse of high cost technologies such as radiology-imaging, brand-name drugs, and many elective procedures" (2009b: 2). As a consequence, to quote another physician, "too many patients have been left 'medically homeless' by our expert-centered system focused on acute episodic care" (Kirch, 2007: 6).

Thus, no matter how thick it may be, the medical curtain is full of holes and frayed at the edges. Like all the other curtains, it should be replaced by one of those beaded curtains used in stores to keep the flies out while letting the people through. **Enough of the double standard in medicine that sets the bar high for other practices while ignoring the low bar for some of its own.**

To summarize the relationship between evidence and experience, beside the generalized science of medical research is the creative art and the rooted craft of medical practice. **Health care—in all its aspects—certainly needs evidence, to challenge biased experience. But no less does it need experience, to challenge biased evidence. These two need to work in tandem, to inform each other.**

The Professional Curtain

To the right of the medical curtain, in the lower quadrant of Figure 5, is the *professional curtain*. Proper professionals draw this curtain hard and fast to separate the certified professionals of health care from the so-called "alternative" practices. It is shown as wavy to indicate that it often proves to be the most arbitrary of all the curtains.

This may be seen as a curtain of inclusion, since it puts non-medical professionals on the same side as medicine. But no less has it been a curtain of exclusion, to keep out practices that narrow-thinking professionals reject even though many people find them effective. Leading the pack in so doing have been the medical bullies—the self-appointed guardians of truth—who lord their science and evidence, however biased, over these practices. (See the accompanying box.)

Medical Bullying

A 1993 editorial in the *New England Journal of Medicine*, entitled "Why Unconventional Medicine?" (Campion, 1993), referred to it as "herbs and crystal healing," and in some cases "probably quackery . . . just the American version of the health spa." Included among these practices were acupuncture, homeopathy, and herbal medicine. "Roughly a third [of such practices] . . . entail theories that are patently unscientific" (usually meaning that correct "scientists" had not bothered to study them), "and in direct competition with conventional medicine" (as if conventional medical specialties never compete with each other).

The editorial concluded that "the public's expensive romance with unconventional medicine is cause for our profession to worry. We need to demonstrate more effectively our dedication to caring for the whole patient—worries, quirks, and all." Good idea. Hold your breath.[1]

This editorial was linked to an article (Eisenberg et al., 1993) that investigated the use of unconventional therapies for health problems in the United States: "16 commonly used interventions

---

[1] A dispute over homeopathy arose in the English NHS in 2006 when Prince Charles expressed support for it. "13 leading British medical doctors and scientists urged the NHS . . . to abandon unconventional treatment and alternate medicines in favor of therapies based on solid evidence." The clinical director of the Royal Homeopathic Hospital replied, "I think what this suggestion amounts to is a form of medical apartheid: any therapy which can't trace its origins to what is called the biochemical model should be excluded from the NHS" [Cowell, 2006]. In discussions with two medical deans a few weeks apart, I mentioned homeopathy. The first word out of both was "placebo." How come homeopathy worked better as a placebo on a friend with shingles on his head whose pain had not been relieved by regular pharmaceutical pain killers? And the next words from the deans were "herbal medicines." These are not herbal medicines. But not knowing what homeopathy is did not discourage them from dismissing it!

neither taught widely in the U.S. medical schools nor generally available in the U.S. hospitals." Thirty-four percent of respondents reported the use of at least one of these therapies in the past year, mainly for "chronic as opposed to life threatening medical conditions." Extrapolating this to the whole country, the authors estimated that visits to providers of unconventional therapies exceeded those to primary care physicians. More telling, the most frequent users of these practices were educated upper-income white Americans between 25 and 49 years of age. Could all these people have been misguided? Or were they just less intimidated by the medical bullies?

Anoop Kumar, a physician who did our health care master's program, has written, "There are millions of people who benefit from healing systems such as chiropractic, Reiki, and acupuncture. Yet these systems are not typically included in conversations about healthcare because we don't understand the science behind how they work. We have the audacity to invalidate the experiences of millions of people because we don't understand it!" (2015).[2] I guess that we can call this ignorance-based medicine.

When I mentioned such alternate practices to a somewhat moderate physician friend of mine, he shot back, "Where's the evidence?" I shot back, "Do you look for it, or even give it attention

---

[2] Classic have been the battles in North America between obstetricians and midwives. Yet in England, 55 percent of babies are delivered by midwives. In Holland, 16 percent are delivered at home—and the figure used to be about 70 percent. Women and babies have not been dying left and right in these places. A gynecologist at the Academic Medical Centre in Amsterdam commented that "I am not interested in doing a normal vaginal delivery and I would not do it as well as a midwife because I will probably perform an episiotomy too early" (Lantin, 2003). An article in the *New York Times* (Bennhold and Saint-Louis, 2014) reported that the NHS had decided to recommend home births to healthy mothers as safer than in hospitals.

when it falls into your lap, let alone try to collect it? Do your journals even give it a chance?"

It is one thing to wonder about conclusions for which there is no supporting evidence, but quite another to dismiss them as if what has not been proved cannot be valid. Think of how much conventional medicine would have to be rejected by that criterion. (A panel of experts in Canada recently turned down a proposal to research a controversial treatment for multiple sclerosis because there was not enough evidence of its success!)

"The randomized trial is a very high bar" [said Morie Gertz, a hematologist who chairs the Mayo Clinic internal medicine department]. "Eighty percent of what I do here isn't based on randomized-trial data." Physicians routinely write "off-label" prescriptions, Gertz says—that is, prescriptions that call for drugs to treat conditions for which those drugs have not been officially approved. It's a perfectly legal and ethical practice, and even one that physicians consider essential, accounting for about a fifth of all U.S. prescriptions. "It's off-label not because it doesn't work, but because there's no good randomized-trial data on it. In the same way, we may not have great evidence that alternative medicine works, but that's very different from saying it *doesn't* work." (Freedman, 2011: 11)

Here, in the accompanying box, is some evidence about experience, from medicine and me.

Samples of 0, 1, 2, and 3, from Medicine and Me

In the 1990s, I was hit with a double Bell's palsy—paralysis on each side of my face. The right one abated quickly, but the left one, more severe, did not. I went to my GP at the time, in a hospital, who marched me straight over to a neurologist, who prescribed a heavy dose of cortisone—which made no difference.

Six months later, in England, a friend suggested acupuncture. As I lay on the table, with the needles in my cheek and a small electric current running between two of them, I was able to wink my left eye for the first time in all those months. Was this a coincidence? (Calculate the odds). A placebo? (Why wasn't the cortisone a placebo?) Experience? Yes. Evidence? For sure—a sample of 1. I conveyed this evidence to my GP back home. His eyes glazed over.

Recently I told this story to that skeptical but open-minded medical friend of mine. He mentioned a common friend suffering at the time from a similar Bell's palsy, for whom the conventional medical treatment was, again, not working. We contacted him, and off he went for acupuncture. His condition abated, too—strikingly, he said.[3]

After this second story, I decided to try acupuncture again (third sample)—I had lived for 20 years with an alleviated but not fully cured condition. It improved remarkably. If you are a physician faced with a patient suffering from such a condition, would you recommend acupuncture? Or will you see its effectiveness only when you believe it?

If you don't believe in acupuncture, consider this. In 1971, Richard Nixon went to China, where a prominent American journalist had an appendix attack. Post-surgery, he was treated

---

[3] I contacted him sometime later, in conjunction with writing this, to discuss his subsequent views. He was more dismissive. "Well, it *was* getting better." (He was, after all, the head of a hospital, although not a physician.) But I had proper evidence: an email I kept from his wife at the time of the acupuncture: "I cannot tell you how much we appreciated your recommendation of an acupuncturist. After one treatment yesterday from a Korean doctor, he is significantly better."

successfully with acupuncture. Here was a sample of 1, widely reported in the American press.

That editorial in the *New England Journal of Medicine* that referred to acupuncture, among other practices, as "probable quackery . . . just the American version of the health spa," was, so far as I can tell, based on a sample of zero. Yet the American Medical Association concluded in a report on acupuncture "that it be the policy of the AMA that non-physician boards should not regulate the clinical practice of medicine."[4] For the AMA, this probable quackery had magically metamorphosed into medicine!

There are certainly irresponsible quacks in uncertified practices—and a few in medicine too. But surely the proper solution, rather than dismissing such practices out of hand, is to certify those people who make responsible use of practices for which we have decades and sometime centuries of experience, whether or not this has been explained by science.[5]

SHEETS OVER THE PATIENTS

Next come the dysfunctional separations between the providers and the users of health care services.

---

[4] The report estimated the number of American physicians using acupuncture in their practices as 2000–3000, while "nonphysician acupuncturists" were estimated to number between 6000 and 7000 in the U.S. Were acupuncture to become a part of medicine, and assuming that American physicians would not be rushing into a practice that the AMA had earlier dismissed as primitive and fanciful, where were all those users of the practice to go?

[5] Just before this second AMA report, another *Los Angeles Times* article on acupuncture (December 2, 1992) showed a picture of a patient receiving a needle with the caption "Doctors speculate that needles stimulate the brain to produce endorphins." Medicine had found a scientifically sounding explanation to legitimize the practice.

When a sheet is pulled over a patient in an operating room, to reveal only what is being worked on—the hip in Room 2, the eye in Room 4—the purpose is functional: to focus the attention of the surgical team while maintaining sterility.

But when such sheets extend beyond the operating rooms, albeit symbolically, they can become awfully dysfunctional. **Underneath every sheet, within every "patient," is a person. Reducing him or her to a condition, let alone to a diseased organ, deflects attention from where it should be concentrated: on the long-term health of the whole person, as well as the role he or she can play in maintaining personal health.** As a prominent authority in American health care commented:

> I fear to become a patient.... What chills my bones is indignity. It is the loss of influence on what happens to me. It is the image of myself in a hospital gown, homogenized, anonymous, powerless, no longer myself.... It is the voice of the doctor saying, "We think...," instead of, "I think...," and thereby placing that small verbal wedge between himself as a person and myself as a person. (Berwick, 2009: 564)

See the accompanying box on "The Military Metaphor of Modern Medicine."

The Military Metaphor of Modern Medicine

To be objective, it has been said, is to treat people like objects. Abe Fuks, former dean of the McGill University Faculty of Medicine, has written colorfully about "The Military Metaphor of Modern Medicine" (2009).

Medicine is organized around specialties, not people or even patients: organs (cardiology), stages of life (pediatrics, geriatrics), techniques and technologies (surgery, radiology), and of course diseases (oncology). In fact, medicine sees the patient as a disease: "The gallbladder in room 6." "He's a diabetic." "The patient perforated her uterus on the operating table"! And so "this thing," "this disease, must be "extirpated" from him or her, in some kind of military conquest: "fighting illness," "the war on cancer," "treatments as magic bullets," "Killer T cells," "invasive tumors" (which Fuks calls "an imperialist, militarized view of malignancy"). There must be a "strengthening [of] the body's defenses," or else "the battle is lost." Fuks added, "The World Health Organization raises the alert levels for epidemics as the Pentagon does for a terrorist attack."

And who is on the front lines of this battle? The physician of course—the "battle" cannot be won without following "doctor's orders." This metaphor casts "the physician in heroic terms, in many instances as the individual responsible for identifying the reified disease resident in the patient's body, naming it and arranging for the means of extirpation or elimination" (p. 5). The patient, namely the person, becomes the "battlefield upon which the doctor-combatant defeats the arch-enemy, disease," while eradicating "the patient's voice from the narrative of illness. . . . When physicians forget how to listen to their patients, they become deaf to their own souls." (p. 8)

Fuks recounts the response of a nurse to his suggestion that she go to medical school: "Yes, I've thought about that. But I don't want to lose contact with the patient."

Within even the most passive patient can be an active person, on whom his or her own health depends, just as within every epidemiologist's population are living communities, made up of persons who can get lost in a sea of aggregated statistics. In fact, many users of health care services are not patients at all. When we seek the advice of a dietician, we may be perfectly healthy; we just want to remain so. And while being called a "client" by the dietitian may be better than being called a "customer," it is not nearly as good as seeing each of us as a person.

Even when a physician or nurse pulls closed a real curtain around a real patient, failure to see the person can impede recovery. (Recall Dr. Warwick's probe into the activities of that young patient of his.) Thanks to the Internet, we laypeople are now capable of asking more pertinent questions, as well as sometimes detecting oversights.

WALLS AND FLOORS BETWEEN THE ADMINISTRATORS

Beside the sheets that keep the providers of health care apart from the people they serve and the curtains that keep these providers apart from each other are the floors and walls that separate the administrators from these providers as well as from each other.

Too often these administrators function on different "levels" (in the hierarchy as well as on different floors of the building) that impede open communication. Much as women are sometimes blocked by "glass ceilings" from moving up the corporate hierarchy, so do **administrators of both genders sometimes bump into concrete ceilings or stone walls in their attempts to connect with each other.** And don't forget the outside walls of the institutions, which are often thicker than they look.

We all know about the *silos* that keep specialized people apart. Well, likewise are there *slabs*—horizontal equivalents of the vertical silos—that keep people on different levels of the hierarchy apart. Each time a slab is added, the communication gap between administration and operations widens, usually at the expense of the operating services.

In publicly funded health care, we find health ministries atop health regions atop health districts atop health institutions atop health services. In private sector health care, we find corporate headquarters sitting over private hospitals that pile managers upon managers—"top," "middle," and bottom (recall that we never dare utter "bottom management")—eventually to get to employees, including the professionals, who provide the actual services.

Competition, market-based or otherwise, aggravates all this, by reinforcing the separations: it encourages the lone wolves, whether individual professionals, narcissistic managers, isolated organizations, or autonomous insurers.

Leadership Apart

Earlier I explained why leadership should not be separated from management: **managers need to lead and leaders need to manage,** at least if they are to know what's going on.

Unfortunately, when administrators remain above the operating ground, on their administrative slabs and in their functional silos, and try to manage by remote control—with all their measuring and reorganizing—the divide between them and the operating professionals widens. And on the other side of this, when the professionals refuse to see beyond their own ground, the problem worsens. No wonder so many people in health care talk through and past each other.

Accordingly, **we can blame the problems of managing health care on uncooperative professionals behind curtains alongside disconnected managers on slabs. Just as many managers have to loosen up, so do many professionals have to open up. Hence enough of professionals grinding in their own mills apart from managers trying to remote control them. Both parties have to recognize that they sit on two sides of the same calling.**

Integrating

We need to mind the gaps of health care, by attending to integration alongside differentiation, to overcome the separations. We discuss these gaps and then consider the coordinating mechanisms that are used, misused, and often not used to integrate the differentiated activities, and then the various forms of organizing that can encourage and impede integration in health care.

MIND THE GAPS

As you disembark from certain trains in the London Underground, a voice reminds you to "Mind the gap." This needs to be broadcast relentlessly across all of health care: **Mind the gaps between health and illness, professionals and administrators, certified providers and "alternate" ones, patients and people, populations and communities, acute and community care, floors and silos layered over curtains on top of sheets, and on and on.** Enough of these separations: **The field of health care will become the system it calls itself when it gets past**

145

its gaps of communication, coordination, cooperation, and collaboration.

Four sets of gaps are shown in Figure 6: (1) *Authority Gaps,* between overall control (by governments, insurance companies, etc.) and the institutions responsible for delivering health care services; (2) *Administrative Gaps,* inside these institutions, between their top, middle, and bottom levels of management, as well as between the silos they work in; (3) *Specialist Gaps,* between the various providers of the health care services; and (4) *Service Gaps,* between the providers of the services and the recipients of them.

FIGURE 6   **The Gaps in Managing Health Care**

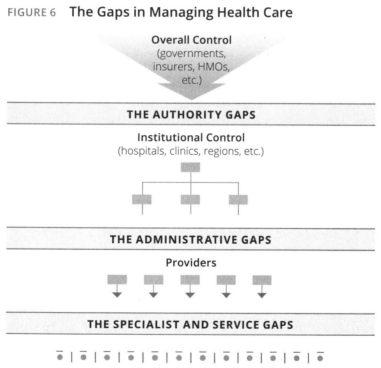

THE AUTHORITY GAPS

Institutional Control
(hospitals, clinics, regions, etc.)

THE ADMINISTRATIVE GAPS

Providers

THE SPECIALIST AND SERVICE GAPS

Professionals and Recipients

Since this is a book about the management of health care, we shall focus on the first two of these gaps, considering how to bring the "tops" and "bottoms" of health care in closer alignment. **(1) The "top" will come "down" when those in administration— managers, administrative engineers, government officials, etc.—come off their hierarchical pedestals, for more direct contact with the operations. (2) The base will be brought "up" when professionals in the operations engage more of themselves in the administration (without necessarily having to become managers). (3) And the separation between the two will be reduced by eliminating the formal "levels" between them** (not by the "delayering" so popular in business, but by favoring smaller institutions and regions where possible). **Eliminating the vocabulary of "top" and "middle" would also help, by challenging all the artificial distinctions of authority and status. Everyone who works in this field contributes and therefore deserves the full respect of everyone else.**

Observe some difficult health care practice—say, an open heart surgery, as I once did (let alone later experienced). Once explained, you will be able to understand it rather easily, even though you will not be able to do it. Compare this with visiting a nuclear reactor. This suggests **another myth: that the system of health care is dreadfully complicated. Closer to the truth is that the complications arise when the comprehensible components of health care are combined into the administrative "systems," whether public or private. In other words, the problem is not in the activities themselves so much as in how we bring them together: something is terribly wrong with how we organize and administer health care.** As suggested in a number of the myths, the favored solutions—merging, measuring, restructuring, competing, being businesslike, etc.—often add to the problem, by dumping oil on the fires significantly created by themselves. So we need to get past these usual solutions.

When Sholom Glouberman and I wrote our paper about the four quadrants of health care, we asked ourselves why the simple combining of activities wreaks such havoc. The answer we came up with is that **the very separations between care, cure, control, and community (as well as within them) create many of the problems of health care, at all levels. There are no management problems in this field, separate from medical problems or nursing problems or prevention problems, etc. There are only health care problems. Many can be alleviated when care, cure, control, and community work together, in the institutions as well as across them.** (See the accompanying box for a pointed example.)

Nothing like a bit of
Crude Encouragement

Some years ago I spent several months attending meetings and observing other activities at a teaching hospital in Montreal (written up in Mintzberg, 1997). Of the 19 meetings I attended, 12 fell into a single quadrant (with no more than a single person from another quadrant in attendance). By far the most frequent were those of the Medical Executive Committee (cure). The Nursing Executive Committee (care) met periodically, as did the Board (community). The Management Committee (control) did include two people from nursing (care), and people from cure and care were included in two other meetings that I attended, in geriatrics.

Only four of the meetings included all the quadrants: two of an ad hoc task force, one of the Planning and Priorities Committee, and one the Joint Conference Committee, which was the only meeting that brought all four of these worlds together on a regular basis. Well, sort of: this was its first meeting in four and a half months! (The Medical Executive

Committee, in contrast, met every other week. At one of these meetings, incidentally, when I commented about how caring a particular head nurse seemed to be, concern was expressed that if I was saying nice things about the nurses, maybe I was getting too close to the administration!)

The emergency room was in a crisis of overload throughout this period, in fact it had been so for several years. Because its chief was on the Medical Executive Committee, this was discussed at every one of its meetings that I attended. So, too, was it discussed at the meetings I attended of the other quadrants. Not much happened as a consequence of all these discussions.

Then the government acted, crudely: it threatened a major cut in the hospital's budget unless the problem of the emergency room was resolved. A task force was quickly struck, involving representatives of all the quadrants and headed by the assistant director of nursing, who was close enough to the operations yet senior enough to get attention from everyone. The problem was finally solved!

Working Like a Cow

So how to bring all the parts together, to get past these gaps—the separations—toward integration? That's easy: **Health care has to work like a cow.**

Some years ago, an advertisement (developed by Anderson & Lembke of New York for SAP Canada) pictured a cow, with lines drawn where cows are butchered. Under the heading "This is not a cow," the text read, "This is an organizational chart that shows the different parts of a cow. In a real cow, the parts are not aware that they're parts. They do not have trouble sharing information. They smoothly and naturally work together as one unit. As a cow. And you have only one question to answer.

Do you want your company [organization] to work like a chart? Or a cow?"

This is a serious question. Please ask it of yourself—daily!

Like health care, cows have divisions of labor: they have hearts, lungs, livers, bowels, and brains. In a healthy cow, each part does its own thing. Yet these work together quite naturally—not seamlessly, mind you (a seamless cow is a dead cow), just cooperatively. And not because the brain orders the lungs to cooperate with the liver, or the heart lords its status over the bowels. Cows just get on with it. Why can't the parts of health care do that? Cardiac arrest teams manage to do so, what about the rest? This is the question to which we now turn.

THE MECHANISMS OF COORDINATION

Welcome to integration, which has to be commensurate with differentiation to avoid separation. We begin by describing six basic mechanisms to coordinate differentiated human work, whether within institutions (e.g., doctors with nurses, administrators with each other) or between institutions (e.g., transfers from acute to community care). While almost all human organizations use all six coordinating mechanisms, health care organizations tend to favor one in particular, often to excess. And in their efforts to correct this, the administrations of such organizations often overuse three others, whereas they should be making greater use of the remaining two.

The basic mechanisms by which people can connect and coordinate their differentiated works are as follows (from Mintzberg, 1979: 2–9; 1983: 3–8; 1989: 101–103):

- Most evident is *direct supervision,* whereby the manager of the unit issues directives to coordinate the work of others, thus vesting coordination in the hierarchy of authority. This mechanism is especially evident in entrepreneurial firms, where the founder calls many of the shots. But it can be found in health care too, for example when a chief of surgery tells two surgeons to reconcile a conflict over the scheduling of operations, or the manager of a community clinic acts like an entrepreneur.

- Most basic is *mutual adjustment*, whereby different people simply respond to each other, as when a hospital nurse discusses the discharge of a patient with a social worker in community care, or the members of a research team examine data together to draw conclusions. This coordinating mechanism is especially prevalent where people have to understand an unusual situation.

And most exacting is *standardization,* in four forms, whereby people's behaviors are coordinated by specific standards.

- Using the *standardization of work*, analysts (work study engineers, etc.) design the work process of operating people to coordinate their work together—on the drawing board, so to speak. For example, a checklist of standard operating procedures (SOPs) is given to the staff of a nursing home to ensure consistency of services to the elderly.
- Using the *standardization of outputs*, managers, accountants, controllers, and the like specify the targets expected of people. A case worker is instructed to see so many people per day, or a hospital has to work within a given budget.
- Using the *standardization of skills* (as well as *knowledge*) is much like using the standardization of work, except that here, because the work is complex, the standards are not imposed by analysts so much as embedded in the training of professionals. Thus, without having to speak with each other, the members of a symphony orchestra can play a Mozart piece together, or a surgeon and an anesthesiologist can coordinate during an operation. By virtue of their training, each one knows exactly what to expect of the others.

- Using the *standardization of norms*, all those engaged in the work are indoctrinated into a common culture or ideology, which encourages them to act consistently, as in clergy trained in the Jesuit order or Doctors Without Borders staff who subscribe to its code of conduct.

As noted, all six coordinating mechanisms are used in almost all organizations, in one way or another. But most organizations tend to favor certain ones, accordingly to their favored form of organizing.

FORMS OF ORGANIZING

There are species of organizations just as there are species of mammals. The problem is that the former are not generally recognized.

Consider two Canadian biologists with no vocabulary beyond "mammal" trying to discuss the best place for the animals they have studied to spend the winter. One who has observed bears says, "In a cave, of course"; while the other who has observed beavers says, "No, in a wooden structure they build themselves to keep out their predators." The other retorts, "But mammals have no predators!" They are talking past each other because they have no vocabulary for the species in question.

Neither do we when we talk about our organizations. So, for example, the manager of a hospital cannot say to a consultant or to a businessman on the board, "You are treating us like a focused factory, but we are really a community of professionals."

Here, then, is a vocabulary to help appreciate the differences among organizations, especially in health care. Four forms are described, called *machine, entrepreneurial, project,* and *professional* (discussed at length in Mintzberg, 1979, 1983, and with these labels in 1989: Part II). Each represents its own way to integrate the various dimensions of organizing.

The Machine Organization

Most prevalent in this world is the *machine organization,* so labeled because it is designed to function like a well-oiled machine (i.e., a focused factory): smoothly, efficiently, and reliably, with operating work that is highly specialized but simple enough to require little training. The machine organization regulates what it can by technocratic controls, of two kinds. One is job specifications—namely the standardization of work, whereby analysts design the operating procedures for the workers—the *how's* of their work. And this is supplemented by the standardization of outputs, whereby these analysts specify *what* are the quantities to be produced and by *when.*

In the machine organization, the hierarchy of authority rules, controls are paramount, "strategic planning" is prevalent (an oxymoron that we shall discuss later), and large scale is favored. Machine organizations are efficient and, like the other three forms, effective only in their own appropriate context. They are not, for example, innovative.

Because this form of organizing is common in so much of business and government—in real focused factories and clerical offices—it has long been considered the "one best way" to organize everything. This phrase comes from Frederick W. Taylor [1911], the father of "Scientific Management," who used time and motion studies to standardize work in minute categories. Since then, the vast majority of management techniques have been designed for machine organizations, both to standardize the work and to alleviate the worst aspects of that standardization (for example, by promoting "empowerment" to compensate for all its disempowering of the workers). Braverman (1974: 87) has captured the spirit of the latter with his reference to the human relations specialists as "the maintenance crew for the human machinery."

Think back to Part I on the myths, and it should become evident that much of the administrative engineering in health care—all that measuring and reorganizing and other forms of controlling—amounts to exactly this one best way: how to make professional operations function like machines.

Reading the popular management literature today, or working with many management consultants, you still get the impression that there is not much out there besides machine organizations. The message is to control, control, control, to tighten, tighten, tighten. Of course, never is this done under the label of machine organization. The controllers and controllees are usually no more aware of this than are fish that are swimming in water.

Water may, in fact, be the one best way for fish, but is the machine origination the one best way for people? This form of organizing certainly fits the factories focused on the butchering of cows, the restaurants that flip a lot of hamburgers, even the cafeterias in hospitals that serve those hamburgers. But how about for what goes on before and after lunch in those cafeterias, say, in orthopedic surgery? There are, after all, other forms of organizing.

The Entrepreneurial Organization

In the *entrepreneurial organization,* **everything revolves around the leader, who makes extensive if rather informal use of direct supervision for coordination.** New organizations, small organizations, and older ones in need of "turnaround" often require this kind of strong leadership—which, by the way, is usually inseparable from management—so that one person can pull things together. But beyond these conditions, such centralization of power can prove limiting. And so, as organizations grow and age, they tend to move to some other form.

The Project Organization

A third form is the *project organization,* **or** *adhocracy,* **where experts work in teams to bring novel projects to fruition.** We can see this in the organization of an Olympic Games or the conducting of truly creative research in medicine and phar-maceuticals. Here much of the power has to reside with these teams, to enable them to learn their way to new achievements, by making use of the flexibility of mutual adjustment for coor-dination. **Try to run an adhocracy like a machine, as some of the big pharmaceutical companies seem to have done with their research, and you kill its creativity.**

The Professional Organization

Most of health care is not about creativity so much as about carrying out highly skilled activities with as much reliability as possible. (Anyone for a creative surgeon—at least for a regular operation?) And this requires a fourth form, which we can call the *professional organization*. (In my early books on structure [1979, 1983], I called it, perhaps more appropriately, *professional bureaucracy*.) It can sometimes be found in business and govern-ment (for example, in accounting firms and regulatory agencies). But **the professional organization is particularly suitable for professional services such as health care and education, in the plural sector—with one major qualification** (to come).

Here highly trained people apply skills and knowledge that are standardized in particular categories (as in medical protocols and school curricula). This renders them largely free of the need to take orders from the managers (direct supervision), or even from spending a lot of time communicating with their colleagues (mutual adjustment). In effect, **they work largely on their own, as most physicians do with their patients and teachers with their students.** Much of the necessary coordination with colleagues is taken care of by the standardization of skills and knowledge—in other words, almost automatically. By virtue of their professional training, the surgeon and anesthetist know what to expect of each other in the operating room, as do the math and physics teachers in a high school. Thus, even when these professionals seem to be working together, they are really working alone, as in the observation by a doctoral student of mine of a surgeon and anesthesiologist who exchanged not a single word during a five-hour operation.

Likewise, when medical consultations are required, often a few words scribbled on a piece of paper elicit a few words scribbled back. That's standardization! In a similar vein, Spencer (1976: 1181) wrote about devoting a few minutes in a mortality-morbidity meeting to a patient with "significant complications or death"—time enough to slot that condition into a category, that's all. This suggests just how standardized can be the work of professional organizations, no matter how complex it is.

If you want to understand the professional organization, simply take every characteristic of the machine organization and turn it upside down: you won't be far off. That is why conventional business thinking—that "one best way," those focused factories—is dead wrong for so much professional work. Remember the story earlier about the MBA who studied a symphony orchestra? Now it can be put into context: he was treating a professional organization like a machine. There, the story was funny; in health care, it's no joke.

> Only recently has medical care been recast in our society as if it took place in a factory, with doctors and nurses as shift workers, laboring on an assembly line of the ill. The new people in charge, many with degrees in management economics, believe that care should be configured as a commodity, its contents reduced to equations, all of its dimensions measured and priced, all patient choices formulated as retail purchases. Their experience of illness is being stripped of its symbolism and meaning, emptied of feeling and conflict. The new era rightly embraces science but wrongly relinquishes the soul. (Groopman, 2009: 27)

In this professional species of organization, power resides significantly with the professionals themselves. As a consequence, strategy takes on a wholly different nature: not a central plan from some metaphorical "top" so much as a collection of individual ventures at the base, most developed by the professionals themselves, whether alone or in small groups: a new treatment here, an altered testing facility there. (Of course, these ventures themselves are usually organized as projects, in adhocracy teams. But once they are established, with the protocols specified, they function within the professional structure.)

But be careful of the standardization of skills of the professional organization. When it works, it can be marvelous. (Just anesthetize me and take out my rupturing appendix please.) But when it fails—when there are unexpected complications beyond the standard categories—it can be disastrous. (Whoops—my appendix turns out to be strangled in some strange way.) **Herein lies the great strength of the professional organization as well as its debilitating weakness: the assumption of almost automatic coordination among the professionals, based on the standardization of their skills.** Under such an assumption, for example, the patient often has to carry his or her information "by hand personally . . . as a sort of 'errand boy' who sews together the various parts of the system" (Adinolfi, 2012). To understand this more fully, let's go back to these three words introduced in Part I.

Categorization, Commodification, and Calculation in the Professional Organization

In essence, **the professional organization focuses on categorization: it functions largely on the basis of pigeonholing, by slotting predetermined conditions (such as an enlarged appendix) into one among its repertoire of standardized programs, or protocols (an appendectomy). The object is not to come up with some creative new way of doing things (a novel appendectomy). That is left to the realm of medical research, or to the art of medicine when the science fails.**

The object is for the professional to get you into one of his or her categories.

Put differently, while the machine organization hardly engages in diagnosis—you ask for a Big Mac, that's what you get—and the project organization engages in fully open-ended diagnosis—try to get a standard campaign from a creative advertising agency—the professional organization mostly engages in diagnosis of a structured and restricted kind: it matches symptoms with protocols.[1]

Because it is the skills that are standardized (by training), rather than the work itself (by analysts), there is some margin of maneuver: the professional can exercise judgment according to the needs of the situation at hand. But that margin is restricted by the prevailing research and technologies that have established the standards—the categories and the protocols.

To appreciate this, consider the continuum that Joseph Lampel and I developed in an article entitled "Customizing Customization" (1996). It ranges from *pure standardization* (table salt), through *segmented standardization* (breakfast cereals), and *customized standardization,* sometimes called *"mass customization"* (the assembly of selected standard components, such as leather seats and the bigger engine, in your automobile), to *tailored customization* (the way a tailor adjusts a rather standard suit to your torso), and finally *pure customization* (an architecturally designed house).

---

[1] "In planned medicine, the most important decisions physicians have to make concern the broad classification of their patients, and what counts in this classification is not the patient's 'individualized' or 'idiosyncratic' profile and symptoms, but those characteristics and symptoms that the patient may share in common with a 'clinically significant subgroup'. This will determine to which subgroup he or she will be assigned. Once the physician has slotted the patient into a particular subgroup, he has already made his most important decision, because the patient's further treatment has already been decided" (Head, 2003: 132). Close, but not quite. Read on.

While most medical practices are rather standardized, as I have been describing them, they should really be thought of as tailored customization. They are not quite standardized because we are not quite standardized. Even a stent needs to be tailored to an artery, just as Dr. Warwick adjusted his own cystic fibrosis protocols to that young woman. Indeed, our communities also vary when it comes to the professional practices of public health. And so, **while the machine organization has to function on the basis of rather pure standardization, and the project organization on the basis of rather pure customization, the professional organization mostly has to function on the basis of somewhat restricted standardization, supplemented by customization, of the tailored kind.**

This is why I objected earlier to perceiving professional services as commodities, with pat treatments whose results can easily be calculated. These treatments have to vary from one recipient to another—beyond, across, and beneath the categories.

The most obvious use of tailored customization is beneath the categories: to the person within the patient. Dr. Warwick was particularly adept in how he probed into her personal life for the sake of better treatment. Across the categories, multiple treatments may have to be applied, which require tailoring the order of application as well as the affects these treatments can have on each other. As for beyond the categories, here is where the conventional practices of the profession break down. **When the protocols don't work, or there are none for a particular condition, novel solutions have to be found. Time to suspend the normal workings of the professional organization and get adhocratic.** Time for that creative surgeon!

Good luck! Habits die hard. Even in much of their research, physicians may be inclined to follow the path of tailored customization—for example, test some medicine in a new population—rather than engage in the kind of truly novel investigations that lead to breakthroughs about the cause of an illness. (In Chap. 18, we shall discuss "A Constituency for Cause.")

And what about calculation? Here is where I believe that Porter and Teisberg made a fundamental error, which is revealed by these species of organization. They based their prescriptions for redefining health care on measures of performance, assuming that the outputs can be conveniently categorized for calculation and analysis. **The problem is that we cannot count the hernias repaired the way we count the hamburgers cooked. Many of them perhaps, but not all.** You never know what will pop up next.

McDonald's might question a cook who took five seconds longer to make a hamburger. But should the Fairview-University Children's Hospital have questioned Dr. Warwick for taking the extra time with that young woman? Indeed, this probably paid off in less of his time needed with her at some later date. (But try to measure that.) Thus, to repeat what merits repeating: **Extensive reliance on performance measures for professional services risks commodifying them to their detriment.** We can never forget the person within the patient, the community within the population.

Of course, Porter and Teisberg were in good company. To continue with the necessary repeating: **Most everywhere in private as well as public health care, authorities have long been determined to categorize and commodify services for the sake of calculating their costs and measuring their results, too often with dysfunctional consequences.**

And not only in health care. As noted, such efforts have often been ubiquitous and catastrophic in education, as governments and school boards have measured in ways that are antithetical to the very notion of learning. Effective educating depends on two things: the selection and the training of the teachers. No direct intervention from outside the classroom—usually excessive curriculum planning and numerical testing—can turn a bad teacher into a good one. But these can certainly undermine the effectiveness of a good teacher.

And much the same applies to health care. To rephrase the central theme of this book: **It can be taken as almost an axiom of professional work that dysfunctional practices cannot be fixed by tighter administration. Some negative consequences of those practices can perhaps be alleviated, but they cannot be fixed. The problems have to be addressed within the work itself.**

Beware of Contamination, Too

These four forms of organizations are of course caricatures. No organization can be that simple. So beware of carrying them too far: they have to be combined in a messy world—tailored too, to the circumstances at hand.

In particular, each form lacks balance, attending only to its own narrow conditions: simple tasks in the machine organization, complex but standardized ones in the professional organization, complex but novel ones in the project organization, and the need for centralized leadership in the entrepreneurial organization. Many organizations need to favor one of these conditions, but not to the exclusion of the others. After all, hospitals need unskilled workers to clean the floors and physicians working in project teams to do the novel research—not to mention dealing with clinical conditions that fall outside their established categories. How often are we sent from one specialist to another when getting them together in one room could solve the problem.

Clinical professionals who are used to working individually in applying their standardized skills may resist working cooperatively when faced with unexpected problems (Kirch, 2007: 3–4). In other words, it's tough to get a professional bureaucracy to work like an adhocracy when it must.

That is because of a phenomenon that can be called **contamination. Whatever form prevails in an organization tends to overwhelm the need for some other form in certain activities.** Try to be a researcher in a pharmaceutical company run by marketing people who think that research is scanning molecules on a screen.[2]

In essence, **a major problem for medical practice is that the pigeonholing of patients into diseases, to be treated by the protocols of specialists, works all too well when the fit is good, and so can become habit forming when the fit is bad. And this habit extends across much of health care**—from physicians having to collaborate with nurses, acute cure having to coordinate with community care, and the treatment of disease having to coordinate with the promotion of health. **Collaborative problem solving can atrophy like a muscle that is hardly used.**

Such contamination can extend into the administration as well, when the managers ape the professionals by trying to work as lone wolves. Managers cannot grind in their own mills the way most physicians can in their own clinics. (Recall the crisis in that hospital emergency room, when the doctors, nurses, managers, and board members were all grinding in their own meetings.) **Most of management, unlike most of medicine, has to be fundamentally cooperative.**

Supplementing the Professional Organization

Thus, **in health care, the professional organization is also part of its problem.** The solution, however, is not to undermine the professionalism of health care but to temper its debilitating weakness. Standardization of skills has to remain its main coordinating mechanism, but this has to be supplemented with other ones.

---

[2] See *The Icarus Paradox* (Miller, 1990) for four trajectories by which organizations that resemble our four forms get contaminated and so go out of control. For example, "Craftsman" companies that resemble the professional form, with "masterful" engineers and airtight operations, [turn] into rigidly controlled, detailed-obsessed *Tinkerers*, firms whose insular, technocratic cultures alienate customers with perfect but irrelevant offerings" (p. 4).

There are five other coordinating mechanisms. Avoid the three that tend to be favored by administrators. I refer to direct supervision by managers and the standardization of work and of outputs by administrative engineers through their reorganizations, measurements, and mergers, etc. All this tends to reinforce administrative hierarchy and to centralize power in the organization, which can drive the operating professionals to distraction as the professional organization is driven toward the machine form.

It is the two remaining coordinating mechanisms that can alleviate the problem. To understand this, let's go back to that cow. How does it achieve such remarkable coordination among its parts? That's easy: its blood carries oxygen between them; its nerves send signals across them; and its life force instills them all with energy. Leaving the blood aside—that's equivalent to the budgets that flow through every organization—the nerves are equivalent to the interactive communication of human networks and the life force is equivalent to the culture of human communities.

These correspond to the two coordinating mechanisms that work outside the conventional hierarchies of status and authority. **The coordination required in the professional organization, beyond what the standardization of skills can provide, has to come mainly from mutual adjustment, namely open communication among the actors, and the standardization of norms, namely a strengthening of their cultures of engagement.** Put differently, **in order to deal with dynamic complexity, professionals have to interact with each other in more robust ways, encouraged by their collective belief in health care as a calling.** Scribbled words on pieces of paper just don't do it.

Mutual adjustment is a fancy term for the informal communicating that takes place to deal with unexpected difficulties. This means talking and especially listening—in the halls, over lunches, across specialties, quadrants, silos, slabs, institutions, and communities—in the form of meetings, committees, and task forces within organizations as well as working groups, joint ventures, and alliances across them. **No one needs useless babbling, but everyone needs fruitful dialoguing, especially professionals to overcome their pigeonholing and administrators to escape their silos and slabs.**

And the standardization of norms is a fancy term for the strengthening of cultures and communityship: to get people pulling together. **No human endeavor, least of all health care, can function effectively without some degree of good-willed collaboration beyond competitive individualism.** To put these two coordinating mechanisms together: when all the players share a set of norms about health care as a calling, beyond their own narrow contributions to it, they are more likely to collaborate effectively through mutual adjustment.

When, however, people and institutions are measured by their individual contributions, competition is encouraged, to the detriment of collaboration. Managers, for example, are driven into self-serving silos, atop self-important slabs. When instead there is a culture of collaboration, within and across institutions, mutual respect has a chance to trump the hierarchies of authority and status. Perhaps we cannot return to some of the practices of old, but we can certainly recognize the price we pay for some of the new practices, and adjust them accordingly.

With all this in mind, let's now turn to the various ways in which health care can be reframed, to carry this field forward—toward functioning like a cow, namely as a system.

PART III:
REFRAMING

NEAR THE OUTSET, I referred to some Italians who complained about their health care, only to discover that their country had been ranked second best in the world by the WHO. I wondered if second best is not good enough. Or do we all just like to complain about health care? Americans likewise complain, but more justifiably, given the costs of their outcomes. The problems seem entirely different in these two countries: in America a market system runs out of control, in Italy perhaps it is the politics that run wild.

But are these problems really so different? I suspect not. When it comes to health care, every country seems to mess up in its own inimitable way, but perhaps for the same basic reason: **Most everywhere, the essential problem in health care may lie in forcing detached administrative solutions on to practices that require informed and nuanced judgments.** In other words, the administrative disconnect may be the real problem everywhere: solutions, crude, crass, or closed, are imposed with insufficient appreciation of the varied contexts in which they have to work. This means that the people who understand these contexts best had better be more deeply involved in determining these solutions.

Earlier I referred to this disconnect as the administrative gap. It is one of several issues that have been raised in this discussion:

- **The Gap Issue:** How to bring the administration of health care closer to the operations, connecting it for support beyond control?
- **The Collaboration Issue:** How to get the different players and parts of health care working in greater cooperative harmony?
- **The Engagement Issue:** How to enhance engagement through the promotion of human scale beyond economies of scale?
- **The Sector Issue:** What are the appropriate roles for the three sectors, especially the plural sector that sits apart from the now conflicting public and private sectors?
- **The Performance Issue:** How to balance the intrinsic needs for quantity, quality, and equality in health care?

In the novel *Shogun*, the Japanese woman tells her British lover, befuddled by this strange society into which he has been shipwrecked, that "it's all so simple Anjin-san; just change your concept of the world." I, too, am befuddled by the so-called system of health care. Here I sit, shipwrecked on the pages of this book. Where to from here?

Maybe it's all so simple, if we can just change our concept of the health care world: to reorganize our heads instead of our institutions, so that we can think differently about systems and strategies, sectors and scale, measurement and management, leadership and organization, competition and collaboration.

As noted at the outset, my field is management (and organization studies) in general, not health care in particular. Given my concerns about administrative engineering, I can now hardly offer my own pat solutions. What I can do is provide some broad guidelines for reframing the managing of health care, while (mostly) leaving specific proposals to those who know the field better. In so doing, this part of the book also serves to summarize and integrate the conclusions that have been reached along the way.

— 12 —

Reframing Management
As distributed beyond the "top"

We have this vision of management apart from what is being managed, somehow above it all, "on top." But on top of what? In business, on top of the pay scale, to be sure; perhaps on top of the headquarters building, too; but mostly on top of that ubiquitous chart that is supposed to depict who has power over whom.

In a widely used model for "transforming your organization," John Kotter (1995) of the Harvard Business School offered eight steps:

1. Establishing a sense of urgency
2. Forming a powerful guiding coalition
3. Creating the vision
4. Communicating the vision
5. Empowering others to act on the vision
6. Planning for and creating short-term wins
7. Consolidating improvements and producing still more changes
8. Institutionalizing new approaches

Every one of these steps comes from that top. Every single one. Can no one else change an organization? Indeed, Drs. Snow and Fleming transformed medicine while being on top of nothing but knowledge. (The Snow story is discussed in a box ahead.)

Think about this top. What a strange metaphoric place from which to manage an organization. **Can people who see themselves on top of their organizations be on top of what is going on in these organizations?** Up there, they are out of it. That is why **it is our heads that need reorganizing, not our charts.**

In hospitals, as noted earlier, the top managers often sit on the bottom—namely the main floor, near the door. Meanwhile, prestigious physicians may sit on top of the pay scale, and of the hierarchy of professional status, too.

Well, if not on top, how about in the *center*: depicting these managers as a hub around which everything else revolves? This is better but still wanting: it *centralizes* the organization, whereas organizations of professionals need to be decentralized.

It can be much better to see management as functioning, not on top or in the center, but throughout. Not to control the organization, but to know it, and be able to respond to difficulties before they become problems. **This sees the organization as horizontal networks of open conversations rather than a vertical hierarchy of structured communication.**

But there is another meaning to managing throughout that may be more significant: **Not only should management be *everywhere*, but it can also include *everyone*.** In other words, some aspects of management can be carried out by non-managers, according to what is known as *distributed management*.[1] **Distributed management reframes practice so that each managerial activity is performed by whoever has the necessary**

---

[1] See Denis (2002: 17–19) on "collective leadership" in health care. To my mind, this is quite different from what Nembhard et al. (2009) propose, which is involvement of the health care "workforce" in the implementation of "transformational leadership" initiatives.

knowledge and perspective to do it most effectively, whether these people be managers, nonmanagers, or groups of both working together. The same can be said about administrative engineering.

Management comprises many activities: controlling expenditures, strengthening culture, raising funds, dealing with government, promoting changes, and so on. (See Chap. 3 of my book *Simply Managing*, 2013.) Some of these activities are naturally done by the people designated as managers, but not all, or even any exclusively. For example, researchers raise funds. And physicians who incur costs can sometimes be best able to control them. As Donald Berwick put it: "Only those who deliver care can, in the end, change care. . . . The outsider can judge care; but only the insider can improve it." Clinicians should, therefore, "stop feeling battered" by the reforms and begin to do something about the problems (1994: 2, 4, 2).

The quid pro quo for this, noted as we have gone along, is that **professionals cannot assume control over certain managerial activities without accepting responsibility for the administrative consequences of them.** Their own interests have to be reconciled with others, at the institutional, local, and regional levels.

Reframing Strategy
As venturing, not planning

Nowhere is the case for distributed management more evident than in the creation of strategies—once we get past the myths about this process.

As discussed earlier, convention has it that strategies are "formulated" at the top so that they can be "implemented" lower down. This process is called "strategic planning," and most of the books on strategy tell you *how* to do it. My book on *The Rise and Fall of Strategic Planning* (1994) tells you *not* to do it. That is because the term strategic planning is an oxymoron: **Strategies cannot be planned formally because they are about attaining synthesis, not just doing analysis. And that requires flexible learning, not formal planning.**

Strategies don't appear immaculately conceived, certainly not from some metaphoric top. Or at least, when they do, beware of them. Most worthwhile strategies emerge gradually and informally, as people learn their way to what works, through trial and error. Such strategies *form* as much as they are *formulated,* with so-called implementation cycling back to formulation.

Show me an interesting strategy and I'll show you a robust process of learning.

IKEA has one of the most interesting strategies in retailing, built around selling unassembled furniture in warehouse stores. This came to be because one day a worker couldn't fit an IKEA table into his car, so he took off the legs. Someone thought, "Don't our customers have to do that, too?" and eventually the furniture business was transformed. Later the company opened a big new store in Stockholm. On opening day, it was inundated with customers. The clerks who took the conventional order slips, handing them to others to fetch the packages, couldn't keep up. So someone swept away the barriers and let the customers go find their own products. Thus was born the IKEA warehouse. (In health care, see Gawande's article "Testing, Testing," 2009b.)

Good ideas. And how about their implementation? IKEA reportedly took 15 years to work out this business model! Of course, management played a key role in this, for example in recognizing, promoting, and organizing these ideas. (That being said, they had to hear about them. How often do such ideas die at the bottom of the hierarchy?)

Strategic learning in the professional organization takes on a particular character: it tends to be highly distributed and rather fragmented. To understand this, consider strategy as it is most commonly depicted (e.g., by Porter, 1980): positioning a company's products and services in the marketplace. In a hospital, the equivalent is the treatments offered to particular kinds of patients.

Successful businesses generally offer a focused range of products or services for rather clearly identified customers. For example, a discount airline may cater to short-haul budget flyers. Hospitals that are specialized do that, too—for example, by performing only cataract or hernia operations. But most do not. They are called *general* hospitals because they offer a wide range of treatments to all kinds of patients for all sorts of diseases (for the good reasons discussed earlier). Such general hospitals do not have "generic strategies," as Porter has identified these: they do not "differentiate" their offerings (except with regard to their geographic location), nor are they "cost leaders."[1] This displeases Porter, and so he favors hospitals that focus their efforts—have strategies, as he sees them. But who cares? Hospitals are about serving people who have diseases, not satisfying gurus who have theories.

In fact, with a little reframing, we can see all this in a wholly different light: **The general hospital may lack *strategy*, but it is inundated with strategies.** Various clinical departments, and even many individual professionals, have their own strategy, in the sense of offering a particular service to particular users. (Recall Dr. Warwick with his own cystic fibrosis protocols and patients.) As a consequence, **hospitals and some other health care organizations often end up, not with one integrated strategic perspective, so much as a whole host of strategic positions.**[2]

---

[1] In fact, such geographic focus is probably the most common strategy in business, too, although it gets little attention in the textbooks, perhaps because it is so common, and less interesting. Consider supermarket chains, national post offices, mobile phone companies, funeral homes, plumbers, and building maintenance services.

[2] See our study, "Strategic Management Upside Down" (2003; or Chap. 10 of my 2007 book *Tracking Strategies*), which develops this point in the study of a university. Across 150 years of its history, it was difficult to identify any period of overall strategic change, even though specific strategies of teaching and research at the professional and departmental level were changing all the time. (For more on strategy formation in the professional organization, see Chap. 11 and pp. 356–361 of this book; also Hardy et al. [1995]. A contrast to this is provided by Porter and Teisberg, who see strategy in health care as centrally driven, much as Porter has seen it in conventional businesses:

> Every organization needs a guiding strategy, which defines its goals and purpose, the business or businesses it will operate in, the services it will offer, and the ways it will seek to distinguish itself from peers. Without a strategy, an organization lacks the clarity of direction to attain true excellence. Without direction and focus, it is difficult even to be truly efficient in operations. Health care delivery cries out for

These strategies rarely come from any administrative center, let alone from some planning process. Mostly they grow from initiatives undertaken by champions in the operations—*ventures* by clinical professionals, alone or in teams. So **strategy making in the field of health care tends to be about venturing more than visioning, and personal and collective learning more than institutional planning.** Thus does a process normally considered to be the domain of senior management end up being widely distributed.[3]

While some businesses have their single entrepreneur—the leader who created the place and guides it strategically—health care institutions tend to have their host of "intrapreneurs" (Pinchot, 1985). Think of all the great discoveries in health care that have come about in this way, for example penicillin, day

---

strategy, given the stakes, the scale, and the sheer complexity of the task. Hospitals and physician practices need clear goals, given the myriad forces pulling on them. They all need to define what array of services they will offer. Providers need to chart a path to true excellence in their service areas, given that their patients' well-being is at stake. Clear goals and strategy should determine organizational structures, measurement systems, and the use of facilities. (2006: 151)

But why should this be; do the authors have evidence for these claims? Perhaps they have it backwards: arguably the great hospitals of America, so many of them general hospitals, are distinguished by their excellence, not their strategies. Has Porter been overly influenced by the position he has staked out about "generic strategies" in business (1980)? "Hospitals (and other types of providers) made the classic strategic error of becoming more similar to their rivals rather than distinguishing themselves. Broad-line strategies have little positive benefit for value" (p. 49). But to whom: shareholders or patients? What's wrong with being distinguished by place—in other words, providing a range of services to a geographic community?

[3] See Bevan (2013) for an interesting exercise undertaken by the NHS. "Change day" was organized as a grass-roots movement to encourage its people on the ground to undertake thousands of initiatives on one day to improve outcomes and experiences for its users.

surgeries, and finding the source of cholera in contaminated water (described in the accompanying box).

Inducing the Cause of Cholera

The year was 1854; the scene was the Soho District of West London. During the stifling heat of August, there had been a handful of deaths from the dreaded disease cholera. Not unusual, in itself. But on August 31, the situation exploded: In a single evening, within a radius of only blocks, doctors reported 56 new cholera cases. By the next evening there were 143, and the death toll had reached 70 and was climbing. Residents started fleeing the district in panic. Medical authorities debated around the clock but couldn't settle on a plan of action.

Among those not consulted on the subject was a 41-year-old physician named John Snow . . . [regarded as a maverick because of his idea] that several diseases (cholera among them) that were thought to be spread via the air were in fact transmitted through drinking water. . . . The initial deaths were all within walking distance of a popular water hand-pump at the intersection of Cambridge and Broad. On his own, Snow inspected the pump, but found the contamination to be negligible—unconvincing evidence for such a virulent epidemic.

Next, he went to the Register of Deaths, and made a detailed list of the past two days' cholera fatalities. But his heart sank as the specifics of the deaths seemed to shoot more holes in his theory. None of the workers at a large brewery adjacent to the pump had contracted cholera, and a nearby workhouse with more than 500 inmates had reported only five deaths. What's more, fatalities had now been reported several miles away, in the rural villages of Hampstead and Islington. . . .

Snow redoubled his efforts, going from building to building, house to house, asking questions of the people who remained.

Finally, one piece of the puzzle fit: He discovered that the workhouse that had largely escaped the epidemic had its private well. Then, another piece fell into place—at the unaffected brewery, the workers told Snow that they were afraid of the public water supply, so they drank only beer.

With a growing sense of excitement and purpose, Snow rode to the outlying homes where the two most recent cholera deaths had occurred. At the house in Hampstead, a surviving relative told him that the lady who died there had a large bottle of water carted to her house every day from the Broad Street pump, because she preferred its taste above all others. Her visiting niece, Snow was told, also drank the Broad Street water and later died at her own home.

The writing pen in Snow's hand poises over his notebook. And her niece lived . . . where?

"Islington," came the reply.

Snow methodically sketched his findings into a rough statistical map of the area. He presented the map—which today resides in a British museum—and his report to the Board of Guardians of St. James Parish. They were finally convinced, and they disabled the infamous pump by removing its handle. Immediately, new cases of cholera started to dwindle, and then disappeared.

A detailed investigation of the pump determined that, more than 20 feet underground, a sewer pipe passed within a few feet of the well. The raw sewage was gradually seeping through the dirt barrier into the drinking water. (From *The Handle,* the magazine of the University of Alabama School of Public Health, Fall 2002: 4–6.)

John Snow was voted in a 2003 poll of British doctors as the greatest physician of all time (from Wikipedia, May 28, 2007).

The terms *entrepreneur* and *intrapreneur* describe people working inside an organization, as did those physicians who pioneered day surgeries. But Dr. Snow did not—quite the contrary. He worked alone, from his personal experiences as a physician. In today's terms, he would be called a *social entrepreneur*. So, too, did a retired police officer on dialysis whose survey of people in the waiting room led to a revamping of schedules to reduce wait times. This story is less grand, to be sure, but the message for health care is grand: **Concerned and committed people in all kinds of unexpected places can improve the practice of health care,** much as so many people are changing Wikipedia every day. Think of this as *open source strategizing.*

"Let a thousand flowers bloom" could thus be the motto for reframing strategy in health care, bearing in mind that this requires all kinds of gardeners, each with dirt under his or her fingernails, supported by administrative people to propagate their successes across the whole field.[4]

---

[4] Jean-Louis Denis (2001, in his report to a Canadian government health care commission, discussed similar "do-it-yourself experimentation" as "a strategy frequently used to promote change." He highlighted "the importance of supporting emergent [and local] change and providing resources and incentives" to encourage it, including "venture capital programs, to co-opt professionals into change management" (p. vi; see especially pp. 11–16).

— 14 —

Reframing Organization

As collaboration transcending competition, culture transcending control, communityship transcending leadership

As noted earlier, when we think organization we usually think machine organization, namely formal structure, hierarchy based on the authority of leadership, clear divisions of labor, everyone grinding in his or her mill, control as rules, budgets and performance standards. All organizations need some of this; many professional organizations need less of it. There are limits to what formal structure can accomplish in health care.

ENOUGH OF THE SEPARATIONS

Organizations cannot function without divisions of labor. No one can do everything; everybody has to specialize in something. The trouble is that we tend to build silos around our specialties that keep others out. And we reinforce these silos when we embed them in hierarchies. Health care, with its hyperspecializations and divisions among care, cure, control, and community, ends up with separations galore, instead of the communication and collaboration that it so desperately requires.

ENOUGH OF THE CONTROLS

Likewise, no organization can function without controls. Nor with an excess of them. As discussed in Part I, administrative engineering in health care has often been excessive. So too have been some of the controls that professional associations have exercised over the behaviors of their members. (I have heard that professional control is making a comeback in health care. Was it ever gone? I hope that collaboration is making a comeforward.)

ENOUGH OF THE OBSESSION WITH LEADERSHIP

To repeat another point worth repeating, the more we obsess about leadership, the less of it we seem to get. So maybe it's time to reconceive leadership too. The cow needs a brain, but that brain does not act as the CEO of its body.

Of course, we are not cows, at least in our collective behavior. We need leadership in our organizations, especially to get them started, to deal with many of their external pressures, and to turn them around when they are failing. But **especially in professional organizations, leadership is neither the heart (the calling) nor the soul (the culture), even though it has major roles to play in reinforcing these. Leadership is not even the** *brain,* **because this has to be distributed,** as noted earlier.

Bear in mind that leadership is a concept rooted in individualism. Say the word and what comes to mind is an individual, no matter how devoted he or she may be to engaging others. Show me a leader and I'll show you a bunch of followers. Is that the best way to foster collaboration in health care? **When we promote leadership, we demote everyone else. Once again, how about plain old management?**

Much lip service has been paid to the leader as motivator, or empowerer, of other people. Do physicians need to be motivated or empowered by administrative leaders? They know what they have to do and just do it (although a little disempowering by the nurses would often be a good idea).

One last word on leadership with regard to hierarchy. Some people have described hospitals as upside-down organizations, with the professionals on the top and the managers on the bottom. In other words, the managers are there to serve the professionals, for example by bringing in funds and ensuring supplies, not to mention providing parking. This is hardly a better way to see things. **Health care needs no one *on top.*** Managers, doctors, floor cleaners, and others all have useful jobs to perform. Everyone should be respected for what he or she contributes, not for the titles they hold. This is the essence of communityship. Managers are no more there to serve the doctors than are the doctors there to serve the managers. Everyone is there to serve health care.

> Mayo Clinic's success is built around a humane idea—meeting the needs of patients. Well paid by a benevolent employer, employees at all levels are able to pursue a value higher than financial gain. Plumbers keep the water systems working so the clinical staff can care for the patients. Custodians clean rooms so patients will be satisfied. (Berry and Seltman, 2008: 125)

ENOUGH OF ALL THAT COMPETITION

Of course, we are all competitive beings. But all of us are no less cooperative beings.

Mainstream economics teaches us about "economic man," for whom greed is good, markets are sufficient, property is sacred, and governments are suspect. As one view of human nature, this makes some sense. As *the* view of human nature, it is nonsense (Mintzberg, 2015b). The notion that some "invisible hand" will right what competition has wrought can be a particularly insidious idea. Look at what it has wrought in American health care. We all want to do better, and we all like to win—sometimes. But so too do we all like to contribute. **The calling that is health care does best when it reinforces cooperative engagement.**

I discussed earlier that health care in the United States has suffered from too much competition, most evidently in its rising costs. But here again, echoing what I wrote earlier, I wish to focus on another aspect of health care competition that is excessive, and not particularly in the economic marketplace. I refer to the competition within and between health care institutions: the battles over beds and budgets.

We have discussed advocacy in health care: the professionals who advocate for their specialties, the managers who advocate for their institutions, the administrators who advocate for their regions, and so on. This may be natural: voices have to be heard, but for real needs, not personal egos. **So let's not celebrate competition in health care so much as recognize that it is necessary, and excessive.**

TOWARD COLLABORATION

"Collaboration, cooperation, and coordination are the three dynamics supporting the practice of team medicine at Mayo

Clinic" (Berry and Seltman, 2008: 65). We discussed *coordination* earlier, about the mechanisms that connect differentiated activities. *Cooperation* extends coordination, by doing it with personal engagement. But needed most is *collaboration,* whereby people join forces in sustainable ways. Just as physicians have to get past their own specialties to cooperate with their colleagues on difficult cases, so too do all the players of health care have to get out of their silos and institutions for sustainable collaboration with each other. (For the NHS experience in this regard, see "The Revolution Will Be Improvised," Leadership Centre, 2016.)

The lack of collaboration can sometimes be shocking in clinical care—from the repeated taking of medical histories to the death of patients who fall between the cracks of established specialties. But how much better is the situation in administration when the managers of care, cure, and control hide away in their own quadrants? Consider, for example, the purchase of equipment. Is this a medical decision about technology or a managerial decision about budgets? It's both, and more—namely, a hospital decision. **Instead of people pointing the finger at each other, they should be pointing their fingers together at the procedures and structures that set them apart.**

Health care doesn't need more measuring and reorganizing so much as better cultures of collaboration that open up the pathways of communication. How about more attention to *architectural* reorganization, namely who sits next to whom, how the corridors are designed, even where the coffee machines are located?

TOWARD COMMUNITYSHIP

As noted, there is no word "communityship" in the English language. But there should be, to wean us off our obsession with leadership and ownership (Mintzberg, 2006, 2009).

We generally use the word *community* in the geographic sense, to designate people who are connected socially in a particular place—the Pilgrim community in early America and the Portuguese community in contemporary Montreal. But the word can also apply to any organization that engages its people so that, in the words of sociologist Philip Selznick (1957), the place becomes a cherished "institution" rather than an "expendable instrument." **A well-functioning professional organization is not just a collection of capable specialists; it is a community of engaged members.** As Kirch put it, "We need to do things to make organization trust run as strong as individual trust" (2007: 5).

Community in both senses matters, because wellness and illness are social phenomena as much as physiological ones.[1] We don't get sick in isolation, whether that be an accident in a car or catching a flu, nor do we necessarily recuperate as individuals. For example, family figures prominently in pediatric and geriatric care, but where is it in the treatment of mental illness? **We need to maintain the health of our communities, geographic and institutional, in order to sustain our personal and collective health.**

In a 2006 paper, Sir Michael Marmot discussed a "support-led model" of health improvement, citing countries where good health has been achieved without rapid economic growth—for example Costa Rica, Cuba, Sri Lanka, and Kerala in India. "Social cohesion, which we may think of as empowerment at the community level, appears to play a key role" (p. 565, citing Sen, 1999). In two of his own studies in Japan, Marmot believed

---

[1] In a special edition of *Making Waves* ("Canada's community economic development magazine"), entitled "Community-Controlled Health Care" (Smecher, 2007), a number of experiences are recounted where local communities took the initiative to establish their own services, even within the government funded Medicare system. In one town, for example, the local people set up the physical facility that attracted primary care physicians.

that lower rates of coronary heart disease were partly explained by "the degree to which people remained within the protective confines of their ethnic group."

Impeding communityship are several of the most fashionable forces in health care:

- the technologies that centralize services
- the mergers that promote large scale
- the social engineering that favors individualistic measures of performance
- the efforts to render health care a business
- the predisposition of medicine to view diseases as going on inside our bodies, apart from where and how we live

What has held the field of health care together through all its years of intense pressure has been the plain old-fashioned altruism of committed professionals, dedicated managers, and everyone else devoted to this calling. As Peter Block put it in his book *Community: The Structure of Belonging:* "Organized, professionalized systems are capable of delivering services, but only associational life is capable of delivering care" (2008: 14).

It is important to understand that **networks are not communities.** Communities go beyond connections, to attain sustainable relationships: beyond coordination, to collaboration. Thus a "community of practice" is not a community in this sense, any more than is Facebook. (If you want to appreciate the difference between a community and a network, try getting your Facebook friends to paint your house.)

Fostering communityship are many of the characteristics that I have been promoting throughout this book (see "Rebuilding Companies as Communities" [Mintzberg, 2009c]):

- an atmosphere that promotes trust
- an appreciation of health care as a calling
- a management that engages itself to engage others

- a structure that is human-scale
- performance measures in moderation, more collective than individualized
- a culture that is robust

CULTURE FOR COLLABORATION AND COMMUNITYSHIP

A few words on culture are in order here, since it is the foundation of communityship. As Kirch described its role in the teaching hospital, "perhaps we are suffering from how little effort we explicitly devote to the culture of our own institutions. . . . Is it a brilliant strategic plan that inspires faculty, staff, residents, and students, or is it a culture that makes them feel fulfilled and valued?" (2007: 2, 3). **Engaging institutions are held together by principles, ethics, and values, not plans, budgets, and strategies.**

Culture is to an organization what soul is to a person. Weaken it, and the energy dissipates. Organizations that work well have cultures that draw people in—that energize them collectively. They see themselves as members—part of an institution bigger than themselves—rather than as "agents" (human resources) of some distant authority.

The fostering of robust culture begins with an attitude that the institution is important, its mission is noble, and all its people contribute to its successful performance. **"I," "me," "they," and "them"—my hospital, their problem—give way to "we" and "us."**

This discussion has reframed the health care organization for the sake of collaboration and communityship. Next we consider three factors that can facilitate this reframing: the practice of managing, the scale of the institution, and the ownership of health care.

15

Reframing the Practice of Managing
As caring before curing

Healthy institutions require a management style dedicated to care, so as to reduce the need for cure. That's why nursing may be a better model for managing than medicine (Mintzberg 1994; 2009a: 245–248).

I am obviously not referring to the boss style of managing exemplified by Nurse Ratched in *One Flew over the Cuckoo's Nest*. Nor am I referring to the belief in some quarters that management is somehow a profession. It is a practice, rooted in context, and therefore learned initially from basic experience on the job. (Later we shall discuss a forum for developing people who manage.)

LEADERSHIP EMBEDDED IN MANAGEMENT

There is an increasingly fashionable approach to managing these days, which you can tell by what it is *not* called: management. It is called "leadership," apart from management—supposedly grander, more noble. Yet watch an effective manger in health care—the head nurse of a clinic, the executive director of a hospital, whoever—and try to separate that person's leading from his or her managing.[1]

In place of heroic leaders who don't manage, health care needs engaged managers who lead. Such managers are part and parcel of their institutional community; they do not sit "on top" of it. In response to a newspaper commentary I published about heroic leadership, a retired manager of nursing wrote to me about her experiences with people "not skilled in understanding the work of front-line staff. . . . [They] managed from a meeting, from their offices, or from their home computer":

> In health care today, the *vertical monopoly structure* is leaving the front-line point-of-care team questioning where is the support, where is the leadership, where is the inspiration, where are the coaches, who really cares? I do not believe there is a shortage of staff; there is a lack of retention of staff. The idealistic, intelligent, youth are not satisfied with mediocre leadership and turn to other professions to have their dreams fulfilled. (Barbara Carroll of Kelowna, British Columbia, in personal correspondence, March 25, 2009, used with permission)

The following box presents a tale of two head nurses, recounted by a gynecologist.

---

[1] See my book *Managing* (Mintzberg, 2009a), which discusses a day in the lives of 29 managers, including seven in health care—from a CEO of the NHS in England to a head nurse of a surgical ward in a Montreal hospital (with full descriptions on www.mintzberg-managing.com). *Simply Managing* (2013) is a shorter version of this book.

The Epidemic of Managing without Soul

(from my TWOG of May 21, 2015, www.mintzberg.org/blog)

My daughter Lisa once left me a note in a shoe that read "Souls need fixing." Little did she know. . . .

A Tale of Two Nurses When we asked the incoming participants in our health management program (imhl.org) to share stories about their experiences . . . an obstetrician told about the time as a resident when he was shuttling between the wards of several hospitals. He and his colleagues "loved working" in one of them. It was a "happy" place, thanks to a head nurse who cared. She was understanding, respectful of everyone, a champion of collaboration between doctors and nurses. The place had soul.

Then she retired, and was replaced by someone qualified in nursing, with a master's degree in management. Without "any conversation . . . she started questioning everything." She was strict with the nurses, for example arriving early to check who came late. Where there used to be chatting and laughing at the start of shifts, "it became normal for us to see one nurse crying" because of some comment made by the new manager.

Morale plummeted, and soon that spread to the physicians: "It took 2–3 months to destroy that amazing family. . . . We used to compete to go to that hospital; [later] we didn't want to go there anymore." Yet "the higher authority didn't intervene or maybe was not aware" of what was going on.

The Management Epidemic How often have you heard such a story, or experienced one? In the work that I do—studying management and organizations—I hear them often (in one week when I first wrote this, four times). And no few are about CEOs in business. Managing without soul has become an epidemic in society—in health care alongside business. Many managers these days seem to specialize in killing cultures, at the expense of human engagement.

Leadership programs these days too often leave people with a distorted impression of management: detached, generic, technocratic. Technocratic detachment is bad enough—numbers, numbers, numbers. The worst of it is also mean-spirited, by bullying people and playing them off against each other. One person, pushed around for years by a nasty boss, said, "It's the little things that wear you down."

These managers focus on themselves. In health care, you can sometimes tell them by comments about "my department" and "my hospital," as if it's theirs because they manage it. And when they get to the "top" of some health care organization, they prefer to be called "CEO," if they are managing a business. They are not. Managing without soul is actually bad for business, too.

HEROIC LEADERSHIP OR ENGAGING MANAGEMENT?

Carried to its extreme, this heroic style of leadership is largely about *curing* through detached interventions: the great one rides in on the grand white horse to fix everything (sometimes on a consulting contract). Too often such people end up in black holes: they fix what isn't broken, while breaking what is. Some seize on a simple formula (for example, that health care is a business), or rely on some technique (like measuring). You can tell them by their use of empty buzzwords, such as "strategic planning" and patients as "customers." See the next box on "Rules for Being a Heroic Leader," which was developed to explain what has been going on in business but is hardly absent from what has been going on in health care, too.

Rules for being a Heroic Leader
(adopted from Managers Not MBAs, *Mintzberg, 2004: 110-111)*

- Look out, not in. Ignore the existing operations since most things that are established take time to fix. Leave that to whomever you did not "downsize."

- Be dramatic, a risk taker (betting with the money and the futures of other people). Do some deal and promise the world, to catch the attention of the press and the money. For example, merge like mad: go after the devils you don't know.

- For senior positions, choose outsiders over insiders: anyone who knows the place is suspect. Bring in a whole new "top team." And rely especially on consultants—they may not understand the place, but they do appreciate heroic leaders.

- Emphasize the numbers. That way you do not have to manage performance so much as deem it. With respect to your own numbers, ensure that you are paid obscenely well, to announce how much more important you are than everyone else. This is called "leadership"!

- Change everything all the time. In particular, reorganize constantly, to keep everyone on their toes (instead of firmly planted on their feet). Refuse to change this behavior no matter what the consequences.

- Above all, get the performance numbers up, no matter how temporarily. Then run, before the real consequences of all this hit home. Heroes are in great demand.

Health care institutions—and businesses too these days—need something quite different: managing as convincing more than controlling, demonstrating more than directing, inspiring more than empowering, above all managers who engage themselves in order to engage others. Put differently, **managing in health care should be about dedicated, continuous, holistic, and preemptive care more than interventionist, episodic, narrow, and radical cures.** See the table comparing heroic leaders with engaged managers.

Heroic Leaders or Engaged Managers

HEROIC LEADERS	ENGAGED MANAGERS
1. Leaders are important people, quite apart from others who do the regular work.	1. Managers are important to the extent that they help other people to be important.
2. The higher "up" these leaders go, the more important they become. At the "top" the CEO *is* the organization.	2. An organization is an engaging community, not a vertical hierarchy. Effective managers work throughout; they do not sit on top.
3. Down the hierarchy comes the strategy—clear, deliberate, and bold—emanating from the leader who takes the dramatic acts. Everyone else implements.	3. Out of the community emerge strategies, as engaged people solve little problems that can grow into big initiatives.
4. To lead is to make decisions and allocate resources, including those human resources. Leading thus means calculating, based on facts, from reports.	4. To manage is to help bring out the energy that exists naturally within people. Managing thus means engaging, based on judgment, rooted in context.
5. Leadership is thrust upon those who thrust their will on others.	5. Leadership is a sacred trust earned from the respect of others.

How to get to engaging management in health care? Managers can start by getting off their leadership pedestals, banishing the notion that they are on "top," and purging their organization of the corporate vocabulary—CEO, customers, and all the rest. They can also make sure that their remuneration sends a message that they are engaged with *colleagues*, not supervising *subordinates*. **Managers need to get down on the ground, to experience the people beyond the positions.**

In one hospital I know, the senior managers sat along what was called "the corridor of indifference," each in his or her own office. Imagine if they shared an office, and escaped it by spending most of their time on the floors, to keep on top of what was happening. **Where there is need for administrative controls, managers would do well to favor "min specs"—specifications kept to be minimally intrusive,** that guide people rather than lock them into bureaucratic cages (Morgan, 1997). Think of the Ten Commandments, the American Constitution, and those five principles of Canadian Medicare discussed earlier. To quote from a paper by Eric Litvak in our master's program:

> Human beings have a natural tendency to respond to increasing complexity by developing increasingly detailed plans, rules, procedures and guidelines.... The problem is that [these] suffocate the inherent adaptability of the system ... [and fail to] take advantage, of ... local knowledge and creativity.... In contrast to this, minimum specifications can provide the necessary guidance to a system while leaving enough freedom for local agents. (2008: 26)

To put this differently, **in management no less than in medicine, scalpels usually work better than axes.**

CHOOSING THE FLAWED MANAGER

True leadership cannot be anointed through the sprinkling of holy water by those on high. Unfortunately, "superiors" usually appoint "leaders" whose leadership they have never personally experienced. **Leadership, as a part of management, is determined by the people who have come to respect the guidance of an individual.** If you want to change the practice of management monumentally, consider the following (from my books *Managing* and *Simply Managing,* 2009a and 2013: Chap. 6):

Everyone is flawed. **Managers succeed because their flaws are not fatal under the circumstances, while their strengths match those circumstances.** There are two ways to know someone's flaws: marry them or work for them. Short of trying to find an objective spouse, let alone ex-spouse, **the best sources of information about a candidate for a managerial position are those people who have been managed by that person.** Selection committees devoid of such information too often choose "kiss up and kick down" people for managerial jobs—ones able to impress "superiors" while treating others as subordinate.

CO-MANAGEMENT

This discussion on reframing the practice of managing has so far focused on managing inside the organization. But there is another side of managing: on the outside, in dealing with all kinds of stakeholders, including users, donors, government officials, insurance companies, professional associations, and local communities. They all have to be kept supportive and satisfied, as well as at bay, so that the people inside can get on with doing their work effectively.

This means that **managing has to be two-faced.** As shown in Figure 7, **looking outward, managers often have to use a more aggressive advocacy style, at least to help secure what their organization needs. But turning inward, facing all the advocates in their own organization, such as professionals intent on getting fancier equipment, these same managers often require a style of reconciliation, open and engaging, to foster collaboration.**

Can the same person do both? Sure, sometimes. But not always. Then *co-management* becomes necessary: **one person (yang) to advocate out, the other (yin) to reconcile in, so long**

FIGURE 7 **Asymmetry in Hospital Management**

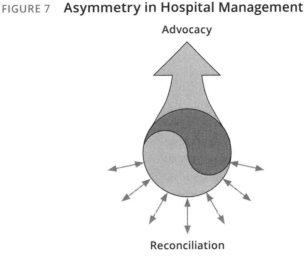

Advocacy

Reconciliation

as the two work in tandem, with the realization that they are doing two sides of the same job.

I proposed such co-management to the board members of a hospital that I was advising (written up in Mintzberg, 1997). As businessmen, they were horrified, at least by the word: someone had to be in charge, they insisted, even if they knew that the particular someone in this job really needed what they called "a number 2." So I changed the name to "cooperative management" and they were satisfied. (Too bad they didn't accompany me when I observed the conductor of the Winnipeg Symphony Orchestra. He co-managed perfectly well with the orchestra's business manager.[2])

---

[2] Written up in Mintzberg (1998; also 2009a: 241–245). Krech et al. have made the case for dyad management inside the hospital, of a "task specialist" and a "socio-emotional specialist." One is "seen as . . . playing an aggressive role in moving the group toward a solution," but tends "to incur hostility and is disliked. . . . Concurrently, a second [person] emerges as a leader . . . highly liked" and concerned "with solving the socio-emotional problems of the group,

WHO SHOULD MANAGE HEALTH CARE?

Great debates continue as to who should manage health care. For example, should the executive director of a hospital be a physician? A nurse? A professional manager? The physician knows cure, the nurse knows care, the professional manager knows control. But is any one of them suited to managing across all this? There are reasons to say no to all these choices. I say no to the question itself.

Professional management has become somewhat fashionable—people with an MBA or MHA. I have already commented on being trained in the abstractions of administration instead of the caldrons of practice.[3] Management, unlike medicine, uses little science; hence it is not a profession.[4] Because illnesses in organizations and prescriptions for their treatment have hardly been specified with any reliability, management has to be a craft, rooted in experience, and an art, stimulated by insights. **In management, visceral understanding counts for more than cerebral knowledge.**

Well, then, if not professional managers, how about physicians? Surely they have the visceral understanding of the operations, plus the status. Moreover, are hospitals not fundamentally about medicine? Yes, to all of the above questions. But there is a lot more to managing hospitals than knowing about medicine. In

---

resolving tensions and conflicts within the group to preserve group unity" (1962: 433; see Hodgson et al. [1965: 477] on the "executive role conciliation" in a psychiatric hospital).

[3] See Noordegraff (2006) on how the very people who have sought to "weaken ... professional power" have themselves "tried to professionalize health care management" (p. 185).

[4] Reay et al., in an article entitled "What's the Evidence on Evidence-Based Management?" found that most articles on this topic encourage the adoption of "opinion and anecdotal information," not evidence (2009: 5).

fact, there are reasons to believe that the practice of medicine is antithetical to the practice of management.

Physicians are trained mostly to act alone, individually and decisively. Every time one sees a patient, he or she makes an explicit decision, even if that is to do nothing. Decision making in management is not only more ambiguous, but also more collaborative. A cartoon appeared some years ago showing several surgeons around an anesthetized patient, over the caption "Who opens?" In management, that is a serious question! Not only *who* and *how* but also *when* and *where,* and especially *whether* to open in the first place. Add to this the fact that medicine tends to be interventionist—mostly about episodic cures, not continuous care—is usually focused on parts rather than wholes, and strives to be scientific and evidence-based, and you have to worry about physicians running hospitals.

This leaves the nurses. Their practice often seems to be more visceral, more engaging, and arguably closer to concern about wholes than parts. They also engage in more teamwork, and their jobs are ones of continuous care more than intermittent cure. So some nurses at least should be more suited to managing hospitals. Sure—but how to get the doctors to accept management by the nurses?

So the conclusion appears to be evident: no one can possibly manage a hospital! Running a complicated corporation must seem like child's play compared with managing a general hospital. Consider the strident doctors, the sick patients, the worried families, the demanding funders, the posturing politicians, the escalating costs, the changing technologies—all embedded in situations of life and death.

Yet people do manage hospitals, sometimes even effectively. So beyond the evident answer to our question is the obvious one: **People, not categories, have to manage health care institutions.** I have witnessed physicians who became renowned as heads of hospitals, likewise some awfully impressive nurses—and imagine how many more if given the chance. One of Montreal's most respected hospital directors was an obstetrician with an MBA earned in mid-career.

My own preference, as I have made clear throughout, is for people who have lived health care in the operations before moving into its management, whether they come from nursing, medicine, physiotherapy, or anything else. In fact, the wider the net is cast, the greater the chances of success.

That is not to conclude that training in management is irrelevant, only that it should be preceded by experience in the job, to build on that. That is what we have been doing at McGill University since 1996—first a master's for managers in business, and since 2006, one in health care, as discussed in the accompanying box.

A Forum for Developing the Managers of Health Care

For years I went around criticizing MBA programs as developing the wrong people in the wrong ways with the wrong conse-quences (Mintzberg, 2004). Trying to create a manager in a classroom—for business, let alone health care—encourages hubris. Devoid of context and removed from practice, such classrooms graduate people who believe they have been trained to manage everything in general, whereas in fact they have learned to manage nothing in particular.

Dysfunctional Consequences Many of these people get into senior management positions, pushed along by their credentials and sometimes by that "old boys" network of fellow alumni. There too many of them depend on tools and techniques, fads and clichés. When they talk about "thinking outside the box," this suggests that they do not. Many favor the fancy processes of strategic planning, which mostly discourage strategic learning. They especially appreciate measuring, because, after all, what else can you do when you don't understand what's going on?

Masters for Managers Eventually, listening to all this, people started asking the question that should never be asked of an academic: "What are you doing about it?" (We are supposed to criticize, not do anything about anything.) Duly chastised, in 1996 I got together with a group of colleagues to create the International Masters in Practicing Management (impm .org). Then, in 2006 the McGill Faculties of Management and Medicine established the International Masters for Health Leadership (imhl.org, giving in to exhortations not to use the word *management* for a degree program in health care), for people from all aspects of health care, from around the world.

The fundamental pedagogy of both programs is this: managers learn best by reflecting on their own experience and sharing their insights with each other. Theory alone, and cases about other people's experience, just don't suffice. Hence both programs are for people in practice who come into the classroom periodically—five modules of 10–11 days each spread over a year and a half—interspersed with various other activities on the job.

Using Work The five modules are built around, not business functions (finance, marketing, etc.), but managerial mindsets: the reflective mindset (managing self), the analytical mindset (managing organizations), the worldly mindset (managing context), the collaborative mindset (managing relationships), and the action mindset (managing change).

We want people to come to our programs to *do* a better job, not just *get* a better job. And so, while we offer lectures, exercises, and so on, as in other programs, half the class time is turned over to the participants on *their* agendas. They sit at round tables in a flat classroom. No need to "break out"—they can go into workshops at a moment's notice.

The whole class, and each group around the table, become communities of learning in their own right. Here the participants reflect on what they are learning, connect it to their experience, share their insights with each other, and consider how to carry all this back to their own workplaces. Perhaps the biggest difference between the two programs is that, while the participants of the business program are understandably there to improve their managerial practice and better their own organizations, most of those in the health care program are also determined to improve health care practice itself.

Various other activities are designed in the same spirit, to *use* the work of these busy people rather than to *make* more work for them. To take two especially popular examples, in *managerial exchanges* they pair up to spend the better part of a week at each other's workplaces—to live in another manager's world. (Thus, a senior civil servant for health in Iceland exchanged visits with the head of the ambulance service in Qatar.) And in *friendly consulting*, held in several of the modules, each participant brings an issue of central concern into a workshop to receive the advice of four or so sympathetic colleagues.

It has been said to "never send a changed person back to an unchanged organization." But management development programs almost always do that. So the participants in the IMPM and IMHL are encouraged to create *impact teams* of colleagues back at work, through whom they can carry their learning to others for consequential changes (see Mintzberg, 2011).

CoachingOurselves.com, a program inspired by the IMPM and IMHL, goes one step further: it takes this whole approach out of the classroom and into the managers' own workplaces. There, in small groups, they download topics of common interest—for example "Crafting strategy" or "It does have an off button"—share their ideas about them, and see how they can use them to develop themselves and their colleagues. This has proved to be particularly popular in health care organizations.

A Health Forum Forward We think of the IMHL as a forum for the improvement of health care worldwide. (Consider it as an effort to bring to fruition much of what has been presented in this book.) In class we have hosted a government commission to do a workshop with our participants. (Its head later reported that this was the best input they received.) In one recent cohort, class members teamed up to form a campaign committee that helped elect one of their own as the international president of Doctors Without Borders. Joanne Liu went on to become the leading player in waking the world up to the Ebola crisis.

The field of health care has no shortage of meetings and conferences. But almost all focus on specific issues, such as health insurance or HIV/AIDS treatments. Imagine instead 35 experienced people (average age in their 40s) from a dozen or more countries, at all stages of development, who are working in hospitals, government agencies, community health clinics, international agencies (such as the World Health Organization), and so on. They meet periodically and intensively over a year and a half to share their experiences and discuss thoughtful changes in health care. The energy we have experienced in this classroom—with so many of its participants devoted to the calling of health care, beyond their personal and institutional interests—is extraordinary.

Reframing Scale
As human beyond economic

As noted earlier, small may not always be beautiful, but it can certainly be engaging. That is why we have to get over our love affair with large scale. Sure, we need to recognize its technological and other advantages (reviewed in Part I), but without being blinded by them. Years of experience with overgrown institutions should have taught us how alienating they can be, especially when it comes to our health.

Not much that I have been promoting in this book is helped by large scale. The larger the institution and geographic region, the less inclined will be their professionals to connect with other specialists and with the managers, and so both to connect with the users of the services.[1] The point is that communityship is especially sensitive to size: we don't easily identify with people

---

[1] Earlier it was noted that governments tend to use health care regions as mechanisms of top-down control more than bottom-up adaptation. Alternatively, expert advisors in the regions could "simply make themselves available to local-level organizations in order to support them, by actively listening, by helping to dissect issues and challenge assumptions, by bringing the right people together and creating opportunities for discussion and learning" (Litvak,

in the thousands or even hundreds so much as in dozens, whom we can get to know personally. That is why some of the most successful manufacturing companies have restricted their factories to about one hundred workers.

How, then, to get past this obsession with large scale? **How about reversing our habits and making small scale the default position? Put the onus on the proponents of large scale to make their case, on human and social grounds beyond just technical and economic ones.** This could not only raise quality, but also reduce costs, by facilitating more of the coordination, cooperation, and collaboration that health care requires.

2008: 40), also, like cross-pollinating bees, by carrying the learning about effective practices from one locality to others. (See also Denis, 2002: 9–10.)

— 17 —

Reframing Ownership
As plural and common alongside public and private

Society's great debate for more than a century, about the influence of private sector markets versus public sector controls, is front and center in health care. Should it be left to Adam Smith's invisible hand, whereby parties that negotiate at arm's length supposedly serve the public by serving themselves, or should the visible hand of authorities intervene through regulations, cost controls, and performance measures? **Health care certainly needs institutional controls and market forces, but it does not need domination by either.**

As described earlier, while professionals coordinate largely through their standardized skills and knowledge, two other coordinating mechanisms are required for the necessary collaboration. These were labeled "mutual adjustment" and the "standardization of norms," one to encourage informal communication, the other to bond people in common cause. While both can be found in private and public sector institutions, they thrive in the more egalitarian institutions of the plural sector, where ownership is often common—in a sense, the property of everyone in a community. This is why we find so many of the renowned hospitals in the plural sector. Once we understand this, we can appreciate **how much more common common ownership should be in health care.**

But rarely do we understand this. As noted in an *Economist* (2010) article about Kaiser Permanente, which operates in the plural sector, there is an option between "politicized state-run systems" and "profiteering private ones." **Health care needs balance across all three sectors which can happen when the organizations of the plural sector, and common property, take their rightful place alongside those of the private and public sectors** (see Mintzberg, 2015c).

The plural sector is not, however, any more of a panacea than are the other two. As noted, if governments can be crude and markets can be crass, then communities can be closed. That is why **careful recognition has to be given in the management and organization of health care to the appropriate roles for all three sectors, not least to constrain the excesses of the other two while cooperating with them.**

ROLES FOR THE PRIVATE SECTOR

Competitive markets would appear to be most appropriate for supplying much of the equipment of health care and many of its physical products, as well as some of its services, such as certain laboratory tests and specialized hospital treatments. Thus, well-known are private hospitals that do cataract operations in India and hernia operations in Toronto.[1] When, however, it

---

[1] Experience in a number of developed countries with private alongside public hospitals suggests that, while the private ones can skim off the easier and more "profitable" services, the public ones tend to be left with the more expensive and difficult services (including dealing with mistakes made by private hospitals). Where people can afford the choice, there can be an inclination to go

comes to pharmaceutical research (in contrast to pharmaceutical development, which carries the results of research through testing to approval), as suggested earlier the plural sector may be a better home for much of it, despite all the propaganda we hear from this industry. (See my article "Patent Nonsense," Mintzberg, 2006b.)

ROLES FOR THE PUBLIC SECTOR

There is no denying the important roles in health care that have to be played by the public sector of every country. First are the services that governments have to deliver directly, or at least fund, to ensure some basic level of access to essential treatments, as well as to promote essential health. Second are the regulations necessary to protect the public from crass and dangerous activities—in all three sectors.

With regard to the pricing of pharmaceuticals, the failure to do this adequately by many governments is beyond scandalous. **A patent is a monopoly granted by the state. How, then, can any state allow it to be used to deny necessary treatments to citizens who will otherwise die for want of what can be affordable medicines? This is tantamount to manslaughter.** Sure, the companies need their profits. But the profits they have been allowed to earn by government complicity will go down as one of the most perverse scandals of our time. Don't swallow the nonsense perpetrated by the pharmaceutical companies that they need such profits to do their research.

And third, evidence from all over the world, hardly excluding the United States, makes clear that governments have a key role to play in keeping the lid on the escalating costs of health

---

to private clinics for less serious interventions and public hospitals for more serious ones. Moreover, there is little inclination in a profit-driven market to attend to mental and chronic illnesses, which, according to Sarpel et al. (2008: 5), insurance companies see as unprofitable money sinks.

care. This will be described later as the role of the "single payer," not so much to control the specific use of resources as to cap expenditures.

ROLES FOR THE PLURAL SECTOR

Key roles for the plural sector have already been discussed, for example in the delivery of many professional treatments in the sector's hospitals and the carrying out of some pharmaceutical research in not-for-profit laboratories. Why do we continue to be beholden to private companies for so much of this research? Imagine what might result if some of the best talent in this field, instead of being siphoned off into developing me-too and erectile dysfunction medicines, devoted themselves to more significant research in plural sector laboratories. (Sometimes even public sector ones. Fiocruz in Brazil, officially public, is a renowned laboratory for such research.)

Moreover, Kaiser Permanente in this sector acts as a single payer for its subscribers, while NGOs such as the Red Cross sometimes act as *single coordinators* across the many NGOs that descend on a disaster site. In addition, many institutions in this sector—charities, think tanks, and so on—support activities across all the sectors, as when the HIV/AIDS Alliance conducts research and disseminates information on treatments for this disease.

Plural sector organizations, aside from private sector markets and public sector controls, require greater recognition and respect from both. But they also have to show greater respect for themselves, by being true to their own callings instead of apologizing for not acting like businesses.

To summarize this discussion of the role of the sectors, **in overall if not exclusive ways, health care is rightly regulated, significantly funded, and importantly cost controlled by governments in the public sector; substantially supplied by** businesses in the private sector; and many of its most important services professionally delivered by engaging institutions in the plural sector. But beyond this, all three sectors have to combine their particular strengths in collaborative relationships. We hear a good deal these days about PPPs (public-private partnerships). We need to hear more about PPPPs that include plural sector institutions. And all of the above takes us to the greatest challenge facing health care today: how to reframe itself it to work as a system—as a cow.

— 18 —

Reframing Health Care Overall

As a system beyond its parts

If a cow is a system while health care is not, can we get it to work like a cow? No. But we can get closer. Since each of us also works like a cow—at least individually and physiologically—surely groups of us, socially, can work more like a cow.

As noted, cows, like us, use blood to allocate their oxygen resources; nerves to communicate across their parts; and life force to infuse energy in all this. The social equivalent of these are budgets, communication patterns, and culture. This final chapter of the book considers how these and more can help health care to get closer to working like a cow. It proceeds under four headings: (1) promoting a system perspective; (2) downloading the whole of health care into each of its parts; (3) connecting these parts through communication, collaboration, and control; and (4) attaining cooperative autonomy.

In discussing these, it is important to appreciate that in a healthy system, the whole is more than the sum of its parts. The word for this is *synergy*, sometimes designated as 2 + 2 = 5. A battery, four tires, an engine, etc., are just so much hardware until they are assembled into a vehicle for transportation. The same applies to the heart in Room 4. It's just an organ until combined with the rest of our parts so that we can come out of that room to exercise our marvelous capacity to recuperate.

PROMOTING A SYSTEMS PERSPECTIVE

When that physician, who in fact headed up the medical committee of his hospital, told me that a colleague who had become director of professional services was no longer a doctor, I should have asked him who he would have proposed instead: An accountant? An economist? How about an MBA? Better still, why not eliminate the position and let the general managers make the decisions about specialized medicine.

His attitude was silly, but hardly uncommon, indeed hackneyed. Such **narrowness pervades health care, from professionals on the ground who can't see past their specialties, to managers in the offices who can't see past their institutions, analysts in governments and insurance companies who can't see past their numbers, and economists in the air who can't see past their dogma.** All of them need to know more and more about more and more to appreciate the system consequences of their individual efforts.

The place to begin broadening perspectives is in the leveraging of health care as a calling. The very morning I first wrote this, I heard an item on the local news about the Quebec government's intention to offer physicians incentives to reduce waiting times in their offices. What a wonderful way to undermine health care as a calling, and as a system: reward doctors for acting decently, as if they are Pavlovian dogs.

This is a bottomless pit: **the more we control to correct, the deeper into dysfunction we get.** Does the heart of a cow bribe the kidneys by delivering more oxygen? No, the oxygen of a cow circulates according to the need of its parts. That is what keeps it healthy.

Now switch to our "system" of health care. Most of the oxygen goes to treating diseases. Medicine waits until we get sick and then dives in with its fancy cures. Good. But better still is to provide health promotion and disease prevention with more of the oxygen.

It is certainly important to treat people who are ill. It is also politically advantageous, since they are an aggressive lobby for greater spending to get them well. In comparison, the many more people who will be getting ill but don't know it yet hardly lobby at all. So **we spend the lion's share of our money treating diseases, whereas more on preventing them would increase our longevity while costing less in the long run.** That's efficiency, as effectiveness! See the accompanying box on "A Constituency for Cause."

A Constituency for Cause

When people "Run for Cancer," the money usually goes to researching cure, not cause: to help those who have the disease rather than to avoid others getting it in the first place. I thought that an ounce of prevention is worth a pound of cure.

Dr. Jonas Salk didn't cure any child of polio. Instead he ensured that no child ever had to be cured again. **We run to find cures for diseases such as breast cancer, but who is running to find their causes?**

Part of the problem lies with medicine itself. It is mostly about treating diseases, and since physicians do much of the research, that is where the bulk of the funding ends up (often with physicians, who, for the sake of the reputation of their institutions, should instead stick to clinical work, where their talents lie).

I asked a surgeon active in breast cancer research about the proportion of funding that went to finding cause. She estimated it to be 1 percent. Sure, she may have been exaggerating, but by how much?[1] The causes of some diseases, such as Alzheimer's, may get more attention, but how many others?

As for pharmaceuticals, there is no money to be made from people who are well, or at least sometimes less money from one-shot vaccines to keep them well. So long-term medical treatments get most of the big money, and that siphons off a great deal of the creative talent that could be looking for causes.

Well maybe: researching cause can be quite different from researching cure—more like detective work, where samples of one can be perfectly appropriate. Find the cause of an illness in someone and you may be finding it in everyone. Recall Dr. Snow, whose sample of two—those two outliers on his map of cholera deaths—clinched his belief that the disease was water-borne. They took the handle off the well in question—that was the cure! (for this well, at least)—and the outbreak stopped.

Have we made any progress since then, at least with regard to investigating cause? Consider this recent report on CBC television. It featured a man with multiple sclerosis who discovered that three of his childhood playmates within a couple of houses on the same block in Ottawa came down with the disease, and thirteen altogether within a 500-meter radius. He reported discussing this with physicians, who dismissed it as likely a coincidence. An epidemiologist interviewed by the CBC commented, "Unless you have a really accurate understanding of what those background risks are [how many people living in that area could reasonably be expected to develop MS],

---

[1] In an article, Servan-Schreiber (2008) wrote (without attribution), "We continue to invest 97 percent of our cancer research funds in better treatments and early detection. Only 3 percent is invested in tackling causes." Some physicians refer to stopping Stage 1 breast cancer from advancing to Stage 2 as "prevention." This is like claiming that the cause of Stage 2 cancer is Stage 1 cancer.

you can't really evaluate whether this particular group is more than you would expect just due to chance alone."

Ye gods! This sounds fancy, but how about doing a bit of extrapolation from that 500-meter radius to the whole country. The cases might number close to a million. (Canada, by the way, has the highest incidence of MS in the world.) So much for cause. So much for the experts. ("It's not my specialty." Whose specialty is it?) See various definitions of experts below.[2] **Where is the constituency to research cause, the health care detectives eager to investigate something with so much potential?** There is hardly any department, it turns out, devoted to living, or dying, communities within the epidemiologists' statistical populations.[3]

2 + 2 = 3: Some Definitions of an Expert

- An expert is someone who has no elementary knowledge.

- An expert is someone who knows more and more about less and less until finally he or she knows everything about nothing.

---

[2] As I was working on this manuscript recently, I received this item in the regular mail: "**YES**, I want to give hope to Canadians with MS by funding the research that is searching for a cure."

[3] The CBC reported further that "the Public Health Agency of Canada recently expanded its chronic disease surveillance system to include MS, in an effort to 'provide an overall picture of the number of MS cases in Canada, allowing us to look at trends over time at the provincial and national levels,' according to a statement from the agency." Populations sure, but how about this community? Some years ago, I heard about an astonishingly high incidence of certain cancers among children in one Egyptian city. Recently I checked on the Internet and found one related article, in the *Journal of the Egypt Public Health Association* (Hosny and Elkaffas, 2002), under the title "Patterns in the Incidence of Pediatric Cancer in Alexandria, Egypt, from 1972 to 2001." The article concluded, "The trends in some cancer types suggest the need of a closer examination of the underlying factors and environmental contaminants leading to the disease in children." Yes, indeed, and what a perfect place to research cause, just as in that community in Ottawa. Yet I could not find any other article, not even a single comment on this one.

- For every expert, there is an equal and opposite expert.

- An expert is someone who knows more than you do . . . but you don't know what that is.

- An expert is someone who avoids all the many pitfalls on his or her way to the grand fallacy.

Was Dr. Snow a good scientist? You bet he was. Have a look at that map in London on which he plotted the places where people died in that outbreak of cholera. But don't just focus on the cluster of points around the well; look also at those two famous outliers, far from the well: they reveal Dr. Snow's systems perspective. How many of today's correct researchers are tolerant of such outliers, those samples of 1 or 2?

A system perspective can begin with a focus on the person in the community, beyond some patient in a population. Beneath every medical patient is a human person, and within every statistical population are living communities. Then, treatment itself can take on more of a systems perspective. Sure, we need to treat "the heart in Room 4." But **medicine has to get past isolated diseases, let alone specific organs, to whole persons.**

> Magnetic resonance imaging aims to visualize pure disease, untainted by the patient or his body, and tissues are merely ghosts on the computer screens of the MRI output. The psyche, totally invisible, and ephemeral from the stance of radiologists and molecular pathologists, has been left behind on the analyst's couch. (Fuks, 2009: 3–4)

Proper medicine, as noted, has been quick to dismiss practices such as homeopathy. Yet medicine can learn from homeopathy about how to consider the whole person. Its initial examination is quite remarkable: it can last several hours, probing into every conceivable aspect of the physiology and comportment of the person, in order to tailor treatment to him or her. "'Activated patients' encouraged to ask questions and to participate with their doctors in reaching the best plan of diagnosis and therapy often achieve better outcomes at lower cost than patients in the more passive modes" (Berwick, 1994: 8). Yet one study reported that patients trying to explain their concerns to physicians were interrupted in 23 seconds on average (Marvel et al., 1999). That's good, because a previous study found it to be 18 seconds! (Beckman and Frankl, 1984). See the accompanying box on "Reframing the Vocabulary of Health Care."

Reframing the Vocabulary of Health Care

1. "Health care" should be especially about the care of health.

2. Every "patient" is a person. (How about *people-centered* care?)

3. But not every person is a patient. (Not when it comes to the care of health, like exercising and eating well.)

4. Yet every person is a provider (we are usually the first responders, for ourselves and our children), while every provider can be a patient (who doesn't get ill?).

5. Also, every "population" comprises communities. (Beyond the numbers are engaged people.)

6. Every pharmaceutical patent is a monopoly, granted by the state.

7. "Evidenced-based medicine" should be called evidence-*guided* medicine.

8. Every established "alternative" practice that works should be called what it is: homeopathy, acupuncture, naturopathy, etc.

9. Medicine is a practice, not a "science" (even though it uses much science, alongside considerable craft and some art). That is because medicine treats the ill, not seeks the truth. Medical research seeks the truth.

10. Management, in health care and elsewhere, is also a practice. But since it uses little science, it is not a "profession," but a craft, rooted in experience and aided by the insights of art.

11. *CEO*, *customers*, and like words belong in businesses, not the calling of health care.

DOWNLOADING THE WHOLE OF HEALTH CARE INTO EACH OF ITS PARTS

Wikipedia contains a remarkable amount of human knowledge. We use it to download information into our own brains. This has broadened our reach enormously. So how about using this as a kind of metaphor for health care: to broaden as much of the knowledge as possible into the brain of each player. Of course, not every player needs to know everything: that would undermine the use of specialization. But many specialists do need to know a lot more about the rest of health care.

According to Wikipedia (circa 2015), a *fractal* is "a rough or fragmented geographic shape that can be subdivided in parts, each of which (at least approximately) is a reduced-sized copy of the whole" (referencing Mandelbrot, 1982). For example, "a branch from a tree or a frond from a fern is a miniature replica of the whole." In a sense, we are made up of fractals, since our DNA contains our own unique genetic code. Shouldn't all the providers see themselves as fractals of the whole of health care? The users, too.

Putting #1 First

If we are to get to a systems perspective in health care, we might do well to put #1 ahead of all the professionals and managers.

You are the most important player in health care; me, too. **Each of us—well or ill, provider or user—is what all of health care is about. We are its subjects and its objects.** Think about how much of our health care is administered by ourselves. As Harry Burns, when chief medicine officer of Scotland, put it in our IMHL classroom: "Health is about being in control of your own life."

So, **to find the systems perspective in health care, look first in the mirror: we are as close as we are going to get.** That is because **you and I are significantly responsible for promoting our own health, preventing our potential illnesses, and even treating many of our own diseases.** We may not be very adept at all this, but who else comes remotely close to doing so systemically?

In the case of illness, unless incapacitated, you and I are usually the first responders, for ourselves and for our children (and sometimes the last responders for our parents). We are often the ones who have to decide whether or not to get help, and if so, where. Or just to treat ourselves instead. (Have you put on a bandage lately?) And after we have been professionally treated, guess who usually has to take responsibility for following up? All we #1s. So we had better get informed. Mostly, however, we are mal-informed, let alone misinformed.

Getting Informed

The more we can know, the healthier we can become. A specialist may be able to claim ignorance and turn to another specialist. But we, being at the beginning as well as the end of the line, often cannot rely on this. Too much of the time, we are at the mercy of our own knowledge. (How often have you come home from treatment in utter ignorance of what you are supposed to do next?) So we had better get informed, or find someone devoted to doing that for us.

Actually, about some things I am pretty well informed. I can tell you about every consequential health care incident of my life, warts and all. Electronic files (at least where I live) are nowhere near being as capable of doing that. (Shall I thank my

221

government for protecting my privacy, even if that may one day kill me?) And where I do have reliable knowledge, I may be able to apply some of it better than any expert. After all, I do exercise regularly, try to eat decently, and floss every evening (even though this too is now being questioned).

So have a look at Figure 8. There I am, holistic me—you, too—in the center, with all the services of health care swirling around me. Maintaining my health is shown at the top, where it belongs, and then, clockwise: detecting illness, diagnosing

FIGURE 8   **Seeing the Parts around the Whole**

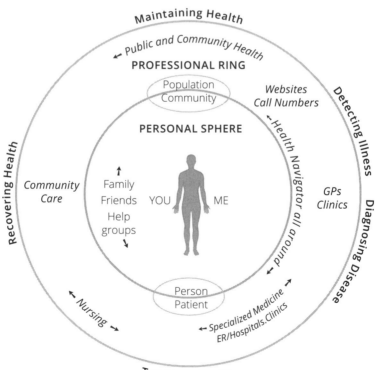

disease, treating it, and recovering health. I sit in the inner sphere—it is labeled *personal*—where I am a *person*, in my *community*. In other words, I am the fractal of this magnificent system—or at least I'd like to be, and it to be. But I need help! First responder I may be, but I am hardly trained for this.

Around this inner sphere is the outer ring of the professional services available to me, from public health through specialized medicine, nursing, physiotherapy, etc., to community health, and so on. Here is where I as a person becomes him as a *patient*, while my community becomes a *population*. It's not enough. The patient is the "single most underused person in health care" (Cutler, 2013).

The Haphazardly Informed Me

Bear this in mind: **While much of the vast array of information that has been accumulating in health care is available globally, every single use of it has to be administered locally.** The good ideas are useless until they get down to specific applications.

Professionals have their systematic ways to get their specialized information: from journals, conferences, medical rounds, and so on. And occasionally one of these experts might pass a useful tidbit or two to me, besides using it on me. But aside from this—which is hit and miss—how am I supposed to get informed about what I need to know?

I go into the supermarket and there sit eggs: omega 3 and organic. Which is better? I always mean to check on the Internet when I get home, but I always forget. What's the use? The answer will probably change soon anyway.[4] But it's not the reliability

---

[4] Or worse, maybe not. A newspaper article I happened to read (Strom, 2012) informed me that agribusinesses represented on the committee that regulates organic foods in the U.S. have tried to get a herbicide approved as an ingredient. What am I to do, short of starving myself (which, as a fractal, I know to be unhealthy)?

of the information that bothers me so much as the rendering of it for my personal use.

There's a massive amount of information out there, some of which I need to know. How much of that part am I actually getting? Is 10 percent a gross exaggeration? And how do I get even that? Haphazardly. (If I missed a radio program one morning, I would not know that I no longer need to feel guilty about not forcing eight glasses of water down my throat every day, only what I need to quench my thirst.) What I get instead are all those expensive ads on the news program I watch, telling me that I should use this or that pain killer. **Relying on a radio program that I happen to hear, or a newspaper article that a friend happens to send, or the television news that I watch, is no way to get informed about my health. Yet, that's more or less all I've got.**

And I'm near the top of the scale: after all, I have a PhD from MIT. (How do PhDs from Harvard cope?) Moreover, I have physician friends I can call about these things. And thank goodness now for the Internet, where I can find all kinds of good information to misinterpret, for example from the NIH and the NHS (https://www.nih.gov/health-information; http://www.nhs.uk/pages/home.aspx). Perhaps better are those wiki-type sites for people to share their experiences with particular diseases and treatments.

The fact of the matter is that much of the time, about matters concerning my life or death, I am overwhelmed, and confused. **Imagine if some fraction of all the energy and resources spent to generate health care information was diverted to figuring out how to get that information systematically into the brains of people like me and you who need it.** I imagine that even 5 percent would be a tremendous improvement.

All the Parts
Medicine has its strengths, which are considerable, also its blind spots, which are likewise considerable—for example, as

discussed, excessive attention to technical gadgetry, the pretentions of being a science and being terribly evidence-based, and a surprisingly widespread inclination to ignore diet and slight so-called alternative practices.

A couple of boxes already discussed the bullying by medicine of these practices, and presented some evidence from medicine and me about successes with some of them. So let me tell you now about one alternate practice that has not been marginalized by medicine. In fact, it is respected by medicine, even used regularly by physicians. It has responsibility for a particular part of our body, where it not only treats diseases, but also attends to the prevention of those diseases. This is not part of conventional medicine, although it does require training much like medicine.

Did you guess what it is? Even people coming back from the dentist rarely get it. Of course, the trick is that I called it "alternative" (which hardly endears me to dentists—so consider how others feel about the label). But dentistry *is* alternate in the sense that it is not medicine, just as medicine is alternate compared with dentistry.

What purpose do labels like *alternate* serve, other than for parochial dismissal? We **don't need put-down vocabulary in health care, or pecking orders of status, or pit bull gatekeepers who deny these practices, much as other misinformed tribes deny climate change. We need respect for every part of health care that works, no matter how unexplained that may be.**

Certainly some of these practices lack sufficient training and certification. But that does not mean they don't work. Medicine once lacked that, too, until it got its act together. So let's bring many of these other practices into the fold—not the medical fold (as the AMA sought to do with acupuncture), but the professional fold—with significant training and professional regulations. Perhaps we need to establish new labels for clusters of these practices.

In an article on "health care reform," Donald Berwick (1994) sought to draw physicians into playing "a central role" in changing the health care system: for example to address "upstream" causes of illnesses (such as smoking) and increase patient participation in therapeutic decision-making. He asked: "How can we, trained as we are in curative care and palliation after the fact, ever really reach upstream to these sources of the ills we treat? Is it, after all, our job to do so?" His answer: "Strong social currents suggest that it may be" (p. 5).

I am certainly sympathetic to the spirit of this. But will it ever be? More to the point, should it be? Instead of trying to change medicine in this way, I believe that we should be recognizing medicine for what it does well, and turn elsewhere for the rest—for example, to create a new constituency for researching cause and to recognize existing constituencies that seem able to treat illnesses largely ignored by medicine.

CONNECTING THE PARTS

If we can get closer to downloading the whole of health care into each of its contributing parts, how can we get these parts to function together—to work more like a cow? We need to consider this at four levels: person, service, institution, and region (community, nation, world).

We have discussed communicating, coordinating, cooperating, and collaborating at some length. I will add a bit to this below, after returning to controlling. I have been somewhat dismissive of it, at least when it draws administrative players into micromanaging the activities of professionals. But there is a key role still to discuss.

Single Payer for Overall Cost Control

As noted earlier, rationing is inevitable in the provision of health care services. Scarce resources have to be allocated, in effective and equitable ways. If there is one clear message from American health care, it is that markets cannot do this. Getting to an operating room for a hip replacement is not the same as purchasing a ticket for a football game. **The invisible hand that is supposed to serve everyone by serving ourselves turns out to be a visible underhand in much of health care when it serves some users at the expense of others. Needed is what is known as a** *single payer.*

In one of his *New Yorker* articles, Atul Gawande indicated that "a choice must be made: whom do we want in charge of managing the full complexity of medical care?" (2009a: 18). He concluded that "we have to choose someone," but he backed off naming who that someone should be. In another article, however, not much later (2009b: 5), Gawande did so:

> Getting our medical communities, town by town, to improve and control costs isn't a task that we've asked government to take on before. But we have no choice. At this point, we can't afford illusions: the system won't fix itself. . . . Government has a crucial role to play . . . not running the system, but guiding it, by looking for the best strategies and practices and finding ways to get them adopted, county by county. (2009b: 3, 5)[5]

Canadian Medicare is a good example of guidance, with its five principles discussed earlier. At the federal level, these have provided an overarching framework for the provinces without

---

[5] "The immediate causes [of an embarrassing shortage of a flu vaccine and other supply disruptions in the United States] are myriad—drug company mergers, production snags, low and high prices, even outbreaks of mad cow disease. But some economists say that they all stem from one central feature of the nation's public health system: No one is in charge. 'We're so concerned in this country about inappropriate public intervention that we're willing to pay very high costs—including shortages—to avoid that', said Marc Roberts, a professor of political economy at Harvard University. In Europe, where governments play a much larger role in managing health care, shortages are much less common" (Harris, 2004).

an overbearing bureaucracy. Unfortunately, this bureaucracy has been created in the provinces, which have sometimes crudely micro-controlled the services provided in their regions. Yet in comparison with the American experience, we can conclude that **for the overall control of health care costs, the crudeness of governments appears to work better than the crassness of markets.** Even in the U.S:

> In truth, federal health insurance is much more cost-efficient than private insurance because of its ability to streamline costs. The existence of multiple private insurance companies increases the complexity of the system and administration costs. At present, the U.S. system is overrun by hundreds of for-profit insurance providers. [American] Medicare's administrative costs run less than 3%, whereas private insurance administrative costs are above 16% of budget [including funds spent to increase revenue by aggressive marketing and billing] (Sarpel et al., 2008: 4).[6]

The role of the single payer should be seen as the capping of expenditures more than the controlling of their use. Earlier we had a good example of this in the box titled "Nothing Like a Bit of Crude Encouragement," about how the Quebec government threatened a hospital with a budget cut if it did not reduce the waiting times in its emergency room. The government told

---

[6] Beside the lower costs and better outcomes in Canada (figures were cited earlier), "In a massive study undertaken by Statistics Canada in the early 1990s, income and mortality census data were analyzed from all Canadian provinces and all U.S. states, as well as 53 Canadian and 282 American metropolitan areas. The study concluded that 'the relation between income inequality and mortality is not universal, but instead depends on social and political characteristics specific to place.' In other words, government health policies have an effect. 'Income inequality is strongly associated with mortality in the United States . . . ,' the study found, 'but there is no relation within Canada at either the province or metropolitan area level'" (Dressel, 2006: 25).

the hospital what to do, not how. Duly awakened, the hospital figured it out.

It need not necessarily be public sector governments that can act as the single payer. Kaiser Permanente, in the plural sector, seems to do this effectively for its members, who number over 8 million in California alone, about the population of Quebec. With regard to capping more than controlling, Kaiser Permanente pays its physicians salaries, and so is able to avoid the "fragmented mess" of so much of the rest of American health care (*The Economist*, 2010). The following box uses the metaphor of bridging to consider the important connections between payers and providers.

Bridging Payers with Providers

In an article entitled "Juxtaposing Doers and Helpers in Development" (2010), Nidhi Srinivas and I discussed the relationship between exogenous helpers (such as international NGOs and the Gates Foundation), that provide generic-type help, and indigenous doers, on the ground (such as community NGOs), that have tangible needs. We described three ways to bridge the gap between them.

One is to *hand over*. For example, an international NGO can provide funding, or information, or training for a community health care clinic. But being on the outside, how can the helper be sure that the doer is making proper use of this help?

So second is the inclination to *cross over*, namely to get into the details to find out, and perhaps control, what is happening locally. Hence "program evaluation" has become a ubiquitous activity for many in the helping institutions, especially foundations. But not being doers, the helpers have to be careful about micro-managing, or else being conned by the doers.

229

Better, therefore, may be the third way, namely to *meet along the bridge*: working together in a relationship of mutual respect. For example, the two sides can brainstorm together about how best to promote better nutrition in a community. This is closer to the systems approach being encouraged in this part of the book.

Liaison and Integrating Roles at All the Levels

Such bridging relationships can be facilitated by quasi-formal positions that connect across the gaps. Thus do hospitals use case coordinators, much as businesses use purchasing engineers who connect engineering design teams with purchasing departments (Mintzberg, 1983: 82–83). These people do not have authority over those they help, and so must rely largely on their wits to achieve the necessary coordination—charm, guile, and so on.

Beyond these *liaison positions* are *integrating managers* who do have some authority, for example over budgets or some other resources. Thus, the unit manager who schedules the occupation of beds in a hospital ward may be able to coordinate the activities of its doctors, nurses, and support staff. Likewise, when dozens of NGOs descend on a disaster site, one may control the distribution of food to avoid the chaos of uncoordinated services.

Health Navigator at the Personal Level

Several new roles of a related nature have developed in health care in recent years. *Nurse practitioner* is probably the most prominent with others being called *health facilitator, patient advocate, community matron* (in the U.K.), and *health activist* (in India) This number of labels should be telling us something, because all of them converge on one message: that at the personal level, people need the help of what can be called *central coordinators* to help them navigate their way through the complexities of health care.

Most of these roles come to the patient from the side of medicine; indeed, they sometimes include the administering of certain medical services, such as issuing some prescriptions. In a CBC radio interview (December 22, 2009), one nurse practitioner described her role as a complement to physicians. (For the breadth and successes of this role, see CHSRF Bulletins, 2010a and 2010b.)

Needed, however, is a broader role on the side of the user—that person beneath the physician's patient—across the whole range of health care services and information. This could be called *health navigator*: a professional fully informed about the person being served, to help navigate his or her way through all the confusion of today's health care. Donald Berwick has noted that "Diabetic patients coached by non-physicians to ask questions when they see their doctors have lower glycohemoglobin levels and higher functional status than those who are not coached" (1994: 8). And Longman has argued that "no patient should ever enter a hospital without having some kind of full-time advocate—a caring, calm, and shrewd relative or friend at least" (2012: xxx).[7] In Figure 7 on p. 222, the health navigator was shown all around the professional ring. He or she would

---

[7] Midwives play a similar role for all the aspects of pregnancy, except that they provide services as well. In business, building contractors play a similar role in construction projects, except that they actually engage the various services (plumbers, carpenters, etc.) rather than just advising on their engagement. In some places, members of the community who have been through a particular illness are enlisted to provide help to others who have contacted it. And of course, sometimes knowledgeable members of the family do all of this informally.

- Get to know the person, in the community, perhaps beginning with something like that first extensive homeopathic interview.
- Remain abreast of health care information in general, as well as of the reliable sites that provide it, and of services available in the community.
- Provide tailored information and advice to help maintain the person's health.
- In the case of illness, guide the person through the intricacies of diagnosis, treatments, and recovery, while providing empathetic support.[8]

Is this role too tall an order? After all, if GPs are overwhelmed, how are health navigators to cope? In fact, this is a main reason why health navigators are needed. GPs are overwhelmed because they have to treat as well as advise. Too often they do the latter unevenly, given the limited time many have with their patients and their limited knowledge of services that are not medical. Health navigators can take the pressure off GPs, while enabling them to focus on what they do best.

Health Activist at the Community Level

Community matters where health care services are delivered. Because we don't maintain our health in isolation, or even so deal with our illnesses, extending the health navigator role into identifiable communities would make sense.

India, among some other countries, has done this, by establishing the role of *Accredited Social Health Activist* (ASHA). The idea is to place a person in each village, to promote and educate for better health, also to mobilize the village in the use of health services, for example for family planning and child vaccinations. They also administer some first aid, improve sanitation, and

---

[8]Apps now do some of this, for example by tracking symptoms, issuing reminders for medications, and even communicating with physicians.

keep demographic records (accessed in Wikipedia, January 10, 2014).

ATTAINING COOPERATIVE AUTONOMY

F. Scott Fitzgerald commented famously that "the test of a first-rate intelligence is the ability to hold two opposing ideas in mind at the same time and still retain the ability to function." Having called for differentiation and integration in much of this book—respect the parts, ensure the whole—I would like to close it with a plea for health care to attain cooperative autonomy.

A *system* of health care, like a cow, should comprise autonomous parts that function as a harmonious whole. Recall that we don't need seamlessness in health care so much as good scams. Accordingly, nothing is served by disparaging specialization for the sake of integration, any more than neglecting integration for the sake of specialization. Nor at its broadest level should health care fail to make use of all three sectors—public, private, and plural—working together.

Cooperative autonomy respects the autonomy of individuals, of institutions, of communities, and of regions, while recognizing that all have to function within a single system. We are individual beings concerned about our own interests, but so too are we social beings whose health depends on the associations we have in our communities. And that, of course, makes us different from cows.

Taken to the broadest level, we live on one planet, which itself has to function as a cooperative system if we are to survive—from global epidemics no less than from global warming. Unfortunately, our planet is sick, and that is making many of us sick, not to mention the field of health care itself. If we can fix health care, maybe that can serve as a model for how to fix the planet.

FINALLY

We can hardly turn our backs on the great advances that have been made in health care. But we do need to face how we have managed these advances.

Much of management these days is sick, especially in big business. Aping this, however fashionable, is not helping health care. The management of health care has to become less distant and opaque, more engaging and collaborative. There is currently too much managing on high as an escape from managing on the ground. And in the professional services, there is too much emphasis on status as an escape from the need to collaborate.

In our lives, homes, clinics, institutions, communities, countries, and the world, we need more fortified care, more connected cure, more nuanced controls, and more engaged communities. This book has set out not so much to prescribe definitive solutions, as to offer a framework that can help those who live the problems of health care every day.

There is an ancient expression that "I believe in it because it is impossible." Not true, in this case, not impossible at all. The French philosopher known as Alain has offered a better expression: "All change seems impossible, but once accomplished, it is the state we are no longer in that seems impossible." Let's look forward to being able to look back on that!

REFERENCES

Adinolfi, P. (2012, April 28). Barriers to Reforming Healthcare: The Italian Case. Health Care Analysis. DOI 10.1007/s10728-012-0209-0.

American Hospital Association. (2006). *AHA Hospital Statistics: 2006 Edition*. Washington, D.C.: Health Forum.

Andersen Consulting. (1997). *Changing Health Care: Creating Tomorrow's Winning Health Enterprise Today.* Santa Monica: Knowledge Exchange.

Andersen Consulting. (1997). *Changing Health Care: Creating Tomorrow's Winning Health Enterprise Today.* Santa Monica, CA: Knowledge Exchange.

Banks, J., M. Marmot, Z. Oldfield, and J. Smith. (2006). Disease and Disadvantage in the United States and in England. *JAMA* 295(17): 2037–2045.

Beckman, H., and R. Frankel. (1984). The Effect of Physician Behavior on the Collection of Data. *Annals of Internal Medicine* 101(5): 692–696.

Bennhold, K., and C. Saint Louis. (2014, December 3). British Regulator Urges Home Births over Hospitals for Uncomplicated Pregnancies. *New York Times.*

Bennis, W. (1989). *On Becoming a Leader.* New York: Basic Books.

Bernasek, A. (2006, December 31). Health Care Problem? Check the American Psyche. *New York Times.* http://www.nytimes.com/2006/12/31/business/yourmoney/31view.html?

Berry, L., and K. Seltman. (2008). *Management Lessons from Mayo Clinic: Inside One of the World's Most Admired Service Organizations.* New York: McGraw-Hill.

Berwick, D. (1994). Eleven Worthy Aims for Clinical Leadership of Health System Reform. *JAMA* 272(10): 797–802.

Berwick, D. (2009). What 'Patient-Centered' Should Mean: Confessions of an Extremist. *Health Affairs* 28(4): 555–565.

References

Best, G. (2007). Leading U.S. Not-for-Profit Hospitals: Lessons for the NHS? *NHS Confederations Leading Edge Report.* London: NHS Confederation Publication.

Bevan, H., et al. (2013, March 13). Biggest Ever Day of Collective Action to Improve Healthcare That Started with a Tweet. National Health Service. http://www.mixprize.org/story/biggest-ever-day-collective-action-improve-healthcare-started-tweet-0

Block, P. (2008). *Community: The Structure of Belonging.* San Francisco: Berrett-Koehler.

Bohmer, R. (2010). Fixing Health Care on the Front Lines. *Harvard Business Review* 88(4).

Bowe, C., and G. Dyer (2004, May 3). Pfizer Seeks a Way to Climb "the Cliff." *Financial Times.*

Braverman, H. (1974). *Labor and Monopoly Capital: The Degradation of Work in the Twentieth Century.* New York: Monthly Review Press.

British Association of Day Surgery (BADS). (2007). *History of Day Surgery.* http://www.daysurgeryuk.org/content/history/history-of-day-surgery.asp

Brooks, D. (2012a, April 23). The Creative Monopoly. *New York Times.* http://www.nytimes.com/2012/04/24/opinion/brooks-the-creative-monopoly.html

Brooks, D. (2012b, June 28). Modesty and Audacity. *New York Times.* http://www.nytimes.com/2012/06/29/opinion/modesty-and-audacity.html

Campion, E. W. (1993). Why Unconventional Medicine? *New England Journal of Medicine* 328: 282–283.

Canada Health Act. (1985). http://laws-lois.justice.gc.ca/eng/acts/C-6/FullText.html

Canadian Health Services Research Foundation. (2001). Myth: User Fees Would Stop Waste and Ensure Better Use of the Healthcare System. *Mythbusters: Using Evidence to Debunk Common Misconceptions in Canadian Healthcare.* http://www.cfhi-fcass.ca/migrated/pdf/myth4_e.pdf

Canadian Health Services Research Foundation. (2002). Myth: Bigger Is Always Better When It Comes to Hospital Mergers. *Mythbusters: Using Evidence to Debunk Common Misconceptions in Canadian Healthcare.* http://www.cfhi-fcass.ca/Migrated/PDF/myth7_e.pdf

Canadian Health Services Research Foundation. (2004). Myth: For-Profit Ownership of Facilities Would Lead to a More Efficient Healthcare System. http://www.cfhi-fcass.ca/Migrated/PDF/myth13_e.pdf

Canadian Health Services Research Foundation. (2010a). *Clinical Nurse*

References

Specialists and Nurse Practitioners in Canada. http://www.cfhi-fcass.ca/ Libraries/Commissioned_Research_Reports/Dicenso_EN_Final.sflb.ashx

Canadian Health Services Research Foundation. (2010b). *Myth: Seeing a Nurse Practitioner Instead of a Doctor Is Second-Class Care.* http:// www.cfhi-fcass.ca/SearchResultsNews/10-06-01/e4e5725f-ae5c-4369-b9c3-dfcd597b1afe.aspx

Canadian Institute for Health Information. (2015). National Health Expenditures: How Much Does Canada Spend on Health Care? https:// www.cihi.ca/en/spending-and-health-workforce/spending/national-health-expenditure-trends/nhex2015-topic6

Canadian Press. (2007, September 18). Quebec Specialist Doctors Get Pay Raise as Part of Deal to End Dispute. CTV News. http://www.ctvnews .ca/quebec-s-specialist-doctors-get-pay-raise-1.256991

Carey, J., A. Barrett, et al. (2001, December 10). Drug Prices: What's Fair? *Businessweek.* http://www.bloomberg.com/news/articles/2001-12-09/ drug-prices-whats-fair

Castle, S. (2016, January 13). Strike Disrupts Medical Care in England. *International New York Times.*

Champy, J., and H. Greenspun. (2010). *Reengineering Health Care: A Manifesto for Radically Rethinking Health Care Delivery.* http://proquestcombo .safaribooksonline.com/9780132371445

Clavell, J. (1975). *Shogun.* New York: Delacorte.

Clifford, L. (2000, October 30). Tyrannosaurus Rx. *Fortune* 142: 84–91.

Commonwealth Fund. (2011, September 23). New Study: U.S. Ranks Last Among High-Income Nations on Preventable Deaths, Lagging Behind as Others Improve More Rapidly. http://www.commonwealth fund.org/publications/press-releases/2011/sep/us-ranks-last-on-preventable-deaths

Cowell, A. (2006, May 25). Favorite Theme of Charles Earns Pre-emptive Riposte. *New York Times.* http://www.nytimes.com/2006/05/25/world/ europe/25iht-royals.html

Cutler, D. (2013, September 20). Why Medicine Will Be More Like Walmart. *MIT Technology Review.* https://www.technologyreview.com/s/518906/ why-medicine-will-be-more-like-walmart/

Davis, K., C. Schoen, and K. Stremikis. (2010, June). *Mirror, Mirror on the Wall. How the Performance of the US Health Care System Compares Internationally.* 2010 Update. New York: Commonwealth Fund. http:// www.commonwealthfund.org/~/media/Files/Publications/Fund%20 Report/2010/Jun/1400_Davis_Mirror_Mirror_on_the_wall_2010.pdf

References

Davis, K., K. Stremikis, D. Squires, and C. Schoen (2014, June). *Mirror, Mirror on the Wall. How the Performance of the US Health Care System Compares Internationally.* 2014 Update. New York: Commonwealth Fund. http://www.commonwealthfund.org/~/media/files/publications/fund-report/2014/jun/1755_davis_mirror_mirror_2014.pdf

Denis, J.-L. (2002). Governance and Management of Change in Canada's Health System. Discussion Paper No. 36. *Commission on the Future of Health Care in Canada.* http://publications.gc.ca/collections/Collection/CP32-79-36-2002E.pdf

Denning, S. (2012, Nov 20). What Killed Michael Porter's Monitor Group? The One Force That Really Matters. *Forbes.* http://www.forbes.com/sites/stevedenning/2012/11/20/what-killed-michael-porters-monitor-group-the-one-force-that-really-matters/

Devereaux, P., P. Choi, C. Lacchetti, B. Weaver, H. Schünemann, T. Haines, J. Lavis, B. Grant, D. Haslam, M. Bhandari, T. Sullivan, D. Cook, S. Walter, M. Meade, H. Khan, N. Bhatnagar, and G. Guyatt. (2002, May). A Systematic Review and Meta-Analysis of Studies Comparing Mortality Rates of Private For-Profit and Private Not-for-Profit hospitals. *Canadian Medical Association Journal* 166(11): 1399–1406.

Devons, E. (1950). *Planning in Practice: Essays in Aircraft Planning in Wartime.* Cambridge: Cambridge University Press.

Dingwall, R., A. M. Rafferty, and C. Webster. (1988). *An Introduction to the Social History of Nursing.* London: Routledge.

Dressel, H. (2006). Has Canada Got the Cure? *Yes Magazine.* http://www.yesmagazine.org/issues/health-care-for-all/has-canada-got-the-cure

Drucker, P. (1954). *The Practice of Management.* New York: Harper.

Economist, The. (2009, May 28). Life Is Expensive: Treating the Sickest Part of America's Economy. Pp. 11–12.

Economist, The. (2010, April 29). Another American Way: Controlling Health Care Costs.

Edwards, N. (2009). *Lost in Translation: Why Are Patients More Satisfied with the NHS Than the Public?* The NHS Confederation. https://www.ipsos-mori.com/Assets/Docs/Archive/Polls/nhs-confederation.pdf

Eisenberg, D., R. Kessler, C. Foster, F. Norlock, D. Calkins, and T. Delbanco, (1993, January 28). Unconventional Medicine in the United States: Prevalence, Costs, and Patterns of Use. *New England Journal of Medicine* 328(4): 246–252. doi: doi:10.1056/NEJM199301283280406

Freedman, D. (2010, November). Lies, Damned Lies, and Medical Science. *Atlantic Monthly.* http://www.theatlantic.com/magazine/

archive/2010/11/lies-damned-lies-and-medical-science/308269/

Freedman, D. (2011, July/August). The Triumph of New-Age Medicine. *Atlantic Monthly*. http://www.theatlantic.com/magazine/archive/2011/07/the-triumph-of-new-age-medicine/308554/

French, R. (1980). *How Ottawa Decides: Planning and Industrial Policy Making 1968–1980*. Toronto: J. Lorimer, Canadian Institute for Economic Policy.

Fuks, A. (2009). *The Military Metaphors of Modern Medicine*. Paper presented at the MSO 8th global conference: Making Sense of Health, Illness and Disease, July 4. http://www.inter-disciplinary.net/probing-the-boundaries/making-sense-of/health-illness-and-disease/project-archives/8th/

Gagnon, L. (2014, November 1). Abut de pouvoir. *La Presse*. http://www.lapresse.ca/debats/chroniques/lysiane-gagnon/201410/31/01-4814636-abus-de-pouvoir.php

Gawande, A. (2004, December 6). The Bell Curve: What Happens When Patients Find Out How Good Their Doctors Really Are? *The New Yorker*. http://www.newyorker.com/magazine/2004/12/06/the-bell-curve

Gawande, A. (2009a, June 1). The Cost Conundrum: What a Texas Town Can Teach Us About Health Care. *The New Yorker*. http://www.newyorker.com/magazine/2009/06/01/the-cost-conundrum

Gawande, A. (2009b, December 9). Testing, Testing: The Health-Care Bill Has No Master Plan for Curbing Costs. Is That a Bad Thing? *The New Yorker*. http://www.newyorker.com/magazine/2009/12/14/testing-testing-2

Gawande, A. (2012, August 13). Big Med. *The New Yorker*. http://www.newyorker.com/magazine/2012/08/13/big-med

Glouberman, S., and H. Mintzberg. (2001a). Managing the Care of Health and the Cure of Disease—Part I: Differentiation. *Health Care Management Review* 26(1): 56–69.

Glouberman, S., and H. Mintzberg. (2001b). Managing the Care of Health and the Cure of Disease—Part II: Integration. *Health Care Management Review* 26(1): 70–84.

Goldberg, P. (2011). *Rationing in the Public Health System in Canada: The Search for an Ethical Construct*. Final paper, International Masters for Health Leadership, McGill University.

Gouldner, A. (1957, December). Cosmopolitans and Locals: Toward an Analysis of Latent Social Roles—I. *Administrative Science Quarterly* 2(3): 281–306.

Granovetter, M. (1973, May). The Strength of Weak Ties. *American Journal of Sociology* 78(6): 1360–1380.

References

Greene, L. (2006, May 2). Money Doesn't Buy Us Health, Study Shows. *Tampa Bay Times*. http://www.sptimes.com/2006/05/02/Worldandnation/Money_doesn_t_buy_us_.shtml

Grenier, A. M., and T. Wong. (2010). The Process of Health and Social Service Reform in Quebec as Experienced on the Front Line. *Canadian Social Work Review* 27(1): 41–61.

Groopman, J. (2009, November 5). Diagnosis: What Doctors Are Missing. *New York Review of Books* 56(17). http://www.nybooks.com/articles/2009/11/05/diagnosis-what-doctors-are-missing/

Groopman, J. (2010, February 11). Health Care: Who Knows "Best"? *New York Review of Books*. http://www.nybooks.com/articles/2010/02/11/health-care-who-knows-best/

Handle, The. (2002, Fall). Magazine of the University of Alabama School of Public Health. http://www.ph.ucla.edu/epi/snow/uab_snow.htm

Hardin, G. (1968, December 13). The Tragedy of the Commons. *Science* 162(3859): 1243–1248.

Hardy, C. (1995) *Power and Politics in Organizations.* Hanover, NH: Dartmouth University Press.

Harris, G. (2003, October 5). Where Are All the New Drugs? *New York Times.* http://www.nytimes.com/2003/10/05/business/where-are-all-the-new-drugs.html?

Harris, G. (2004, October 31). In American Health Care, Drug Shortages Are Chronic. *New York Times.* http://www.nytimes.com/2004/10/31/weekinreview/in-american-health-care-drug-shortages-are-chronic.html

Head, S. (2003). *The New Ruthless Economy: Work and Power in the Digital Age.* Oxford: Oxford University Press.

Hediger, V., T. Lambert, and M. Mourshed. (2007). Private Solutions for Health Care in the Gulf. *McKinsey Quarterly*, Special Edition: 49–58.

Herzlinger, R. (2006, May). Why Innovation in Health Care Is So Hard. *Harvard Business Review* 84(5): 58–66.

Herzlinger, R. (2007). Who Killed Healthcare? New York: McGraw-Hill.

Himmelstein, D., and S. Woolhandler. (2016, January). Public Health's Falling Share of US Health Spending. *American Journal of Public Health* 106(1): 56–57.

Hitchens, C. (1998, August). Bitter Medicine. *Vanity Fair.*

Hodgson, R., D. Levinson, and A. Zaleznik. *(1965). The Executive Role Constellation: An Analysis of Personality and Role Relations.* Cambridge, MA: Harvard Business School Press.

References

Hosny, G., and S. Elkaffas. (2002). Patterns in the Incidence of Pediatric Cancer in Alexandria, Egypt, from 1972 to 2001. *Journal of the Egypt Public Health Association* 77(5–6): 451–468.

Howey, C. (1993). Summary of *Getting Things Done: The ABCs of Time Management* by Edwin C. Bliss. New York, Scribner, 1976. http://www.refresher.com/!chhtime.html

Jauhar, S. (2010, January 22). One Thing After Another: Review of Atul Gawande's "The Checklist Manifesto." *Sunday Book Review, New York Times.* http://www.nytimes.com/2010/01/24/books/review/Jauhar-t.html?

Jauhar, S. (2015, July 22). Giving Doctors Grades. *New York Times.* http://www.nytimes.com/2015/07/22/opinion/giving-doctors-grades.html

Kaiser Family Foundation. (2011, April). *Health Care Spending in the United States and Selected OECD Countries.* http://www.kff.org/insurance/snapshot/OECD042111.cfm

Kantola, A., and H. Seeck. (2011). Dissemination of Management into Politics: Michael Porter and the Political Uses of Management Consulting. *Management Learning* 42(1): 25–47. doi: 10.1177/1350507610382489

Kaplan, A. (1964). *The Conduct of Inquiry: Methodology for Behavioral Science.* San Francisco: Chandler.

Kaplan, R., and D. Norton (1992, January/February). The Balanced Scorecard: Measures That Drive Performance. *Harvard Business Review* 70(1): 71–79. https://hbr.org/2005/07/the-balanced-scorecard-measures-that-drive-performance

Kaplan, R., and M. Porter. (2011, September). How to Solve the Cost Crisis in Health Care. *Harvard Business Review* 89(9): 47–64. https://hbr.org/2011/09/how-to-solve-the-cost-crisis-in-health-care

Kennedy, J., and Pomerantz, G. (1986, July 30). USFL Is Awarded $1 in Suit Against NFL. *Washington Post.*

Kirch, D. G. (2007). *President's Address: Culture and the Courage to Change.* Paper presented at the Association of American Medical Colleges, 118th annual meeting. https://www.aamc.org/download/169722/data/kirchspeech2007.pdf

Kotter, J. (1990, May/June). What Leaders Really Do. *Harvard Business Review* 68(3): 103–111.

Kotter, J. (1995, March/April) Leading Change: Why Transformation Efforts Fail. *Harvard Business Review* 73(2).

Krech, D., R. Crutchfield, and E. Ballachey. (1962). *Individual in Society: A Textbook of Social Psychology.* New York: McGraw-Hill.

Krugman, P. (2011, April 21). Patients Are Not Consumers. *New York Times.*

References

http://www.nytimes.com/2011/04/22/opinion/22krugman.html

Kumar, A. (2015, August 29). Every Patient's Experience Is Valid. Personal Blog: Anoop Kumar, M.D. http://www.anoopkumar.com/blog//patient-experience

Kushlick A. (1975, April 26). Health Care Evaluation Research Team (Wessex, Regional Health Authority, England), [untitled] paper presented to the Annual Conference of the British Society for the Study of Mental Subnormality.

Lantin, B. (2003, January 24). Home Births Without Hazards. *The Telegraph*.

Lawrence, P., and J. Lorsch. (1967). Differentiation and Integration in Complex Organizations. *Administrative Science Quarterly*. Cornell University, Johnson Graduate School of Management.

Leadership Centre. (2016, February). *The Revolution Will Be Improvised Part II*. A report by The Leadership Centre for The Systems Leadership Steering Group. http://www.thinklocalactpersonal.org.uk/_assets/News/The_Revolution_will_be_Improvised_Part_II.pdf

Light, D. (1994, October 29). Managed Care: False and Real Solutions. *The Lancet* 344(8931): 1197–1199.

Litvak, E. (2008). *Governing Population-Oriented Health Systems*. Final paper, International Masters for Health Leadership, McGill University.

Longman, P. (2012). *Best Care Anywhere*. San Francisco: Berrett-Koehler.

Macmillan, A. (2006, April 28). Health Care, Swedish Style. *CBC News*. http://www.cbc.ca/news2/reportsfromabroad/macmillan/20060428.html

Magder, J. (2007, September 18). Quebec Reaches Deal with Specialists. *Montreal Gazette*.

Maltz, M. (1997). *Bridging Gaps in Police Crime Data: Executive Summary*. Discussion paper, BJS Fellow Program, Bureau of Justice Statistics. Washington, D.C.: U.S. Department of Justice, Office of Justice Programs.

Mandelbrot, B. (1982). *The Fractal Geometry of Nature*. San Francisco: W.H. Freeman.

Marmor, T. (2007). *Fads, Fallacies and Foolishness in Medical Care Management and Policy*. Singapore: World Scientific.

Marmot, M. (2006). Health in an Unequal World: Social Circumstances, Biology and Disease. *Clinical Medicine (London, England)* 6(6).

Marvel, M., R. Epstein, K. Flowers, and H. Beckman. (1999). Soliciting the Patient's Agenda: Have We Improved? *JAMA* 281(3): 283–287.

McKee, M. (2001). Measuring the Efficiency of Health Systems. *British Medical Journal* 323(7308): 295–296.

References

Meindl, J., S. Ehrlich, and J. Dukerich. (1985). The Romance of Leadership. *Administrative Science Quarterly* 30: 78–102.

Melhado, E. (2006). Health Planning in the United States and the Decline of Public-Interest Policymaking. *Milbank Quarterly* 84(2): 359–440.

Miller, D. (1990). *The Icarus Paradox: How Exceptional Companies Bring About Their Own Downfall: New Lessons in the Dynamics of Corporate Success, Decline, and Renewal.* New York: HarperBusiness.

Mintzberg, H. (1973). *The Nature of Managerial Work.* New York: Harper & Row.

Mintzberg, H. (1975). *Impediments to the Use of Management Information.* A study carried out on behalf of the National Association of Accountants, New York, N.Y. and the Society of Industrial Accountants of Canada, Hamilton, Ontario, Canada.

Mintzberg, H. (1979). *The Structuring of Organizations.* Upper Saddle River, NJ: Prentice Hall.

Mintzberg, H. (1982, October). A Note on That Dirty Word Efficiency. *Interfaces.*

Mintzberg, H. (1983). *Structure in Fives: Designing Effective Organizations.* Upper Saddle River, NJ: Prentice Hall.

Mintzberg, H. (1989). *Mintzberg on Management: Inside Our Strange World of Organizations.* New York: Free Press.

Mintzberg, H. (1994, September). Managing as Blended Care. *Journal of Nursing Administration.*

Mintzberg, H. (1996). Managing Government, Governing Management. *Harvard Business Review* 74(3): 75.

Mintzberg, H. (1997). Toward Healthier Hospitals. *Health Care Management Review* 22(4): 9.

Mintzberg, H. (1998, November/December). Covert Leadership: The Art of Managing Professionals. *Harvard Business Review.* https://hbr.org/1998/11/covert-leadership-notes-on-managing-professionals/ar/1

Mintzberg, H. (2001, Spring). The Yin and Yang of Managing. *Organizational Dynamics.*

Mintzberg, H. (2003, December). Strategic Management Upside Down. *Canadian Journal of Administrative Sciences.*

Mintzberg, H. (2004). *Managers Not MBAs.* San Francisco: Berrett-Koehler.

Mintzberg, H. (2006a, October 23). Community-ship is the Answer. *Financial Times.*

Mintzberg, H. (2006b). Patent Nonsense: Evidence Tells of an Industry Out of Social Control. *Canadian Medical Association Journal* 175(4): 374.

References

Mintzberg, H. (2007). *Tracking Strategies: Towards a General Theory of Strategy Formation*. New York: Oxford University Press.

Mintzberg, H. (2009a). *Managing*. San Francisco: Berrett-Koehler.

Mintzberg, H. (2009b, 30 November). No More Executive Bonuses. *Wall Street Journal*.

Mintzberg, H. (2009c, July/August). Rebuilding Companies as Communities. *Harvard Business Review*.

Mintzberg, H. (2011). From Management Development to Organization Development with IMpact. *OD Practitioner* 43(3).

Mintzberg, H. (2012). Managing the Myths of Health Care. *World Hospitals and Health Services* 48(3).

Mintzberg, H. (2013). *Simply Managing*. San Francisco: Berrett-Koehler.

Mintzberg, H. (2105a, May 21). The Epidemic of Managing Without Soul. *TWOG*. www.mintzberg.org/blog

Mintzberg, H. (2015b). *Rebalancing Society: Radical Renewal Beyond Left, Right, and Center*. San Francisco: Berrett-Koehler.

Mintzberg, H. (2015c, Summer). Time for the Plural Sector. *Stanford Social Innovation Review*. http://ssir.org/articles/entry/time_for_the_plural_sector

Mintzberg, H. (2016a, February 24). Ne réformons pas le système de santé en le mettant en pieces. *Le Devoir*.

Mintzberg, H. (2016b, February 25). Opinion: Let's Not Fix Health Care by Breaking It. *Montreal Gazette*. [Interview with Phil Carpenter.]

Mintzberg, H., and J. Lampel (1996, Fall). Customizing Customization. *Sloan Management Review*.

Mintzberg, H., R. Molz, E. Raufflet, P. Sloan, C. Abdallah, R. Bercuvitz, and C. Tzeng. (2005). The Invisible World of Association. *Leader to Leader* 36: 37–45.

Mintzberg, H., and N. Srinivas (2010). Juxtaposing Doers and Helpers in Development. *Community Development Journal* 45(1): 39–57.

Mitchell, W., A. Venkatraman, J. Banaszak-Hall, and W. Bert. (2004). *The Commercialization of Nursing Home Care: Does For-Profit Cost-Control Mean Lower Quality or Do Corporations Provide the Best of Both Worlds?* Duke Center for the Advancement of Social Entrepreneurship. http://www.caseatduke.org/documents/FPvNP_NursingHomes_mitchell.pdf

Mitroff, L. (1974). *The Subjective Side of Science: A Philosophical Inquiry into the Psychology of the Apollo Moon Scientists*. Amsterdam: Elsevier.

Morgan, G. (1997). *Images of Organization* (2nd ed.). Newbury Park, CA: Sage.

Nembhard, I., J. Alexander, T. Hoff, and R. Ramanujam. (2009). Why Does the Quality of Health Care Continue to Lag? Insights from Management Research. *Academy of Management Perspectives* 23(1): 24–42.

Neustadt, R. (1960). *Presidential Power and the Modern Presidents: The Politics of Leadership.* New York: Wiley.

Noordegraff, M. (2006). Professional Management of Professionals. In *De-professionalisation and Reprofessionalisation in Care and Welfare,* ed. J. Duyvendak, T. Knijn, and M. Kremer. Amsterdam: Amsterdam University Press.

Okma, K., T. Cheng, D. Chinitz, L. Crivelli, M. Lim, H. Maarse, and M. Labra. (2010). Six Countries, Six Health Reform Models? Health Care Reform in Chile, Israel, Singapore, Switzerland, Taiwan and The Netherlands. *Journal of Comparative Policy Analysis: Research and Practice* 12(1–2): 75–113.

Page, L. (2011, June). Private Equity Funds Are Changing the Face of U.S. Hospitals. *Becker's Hospital Review* no. 5. http://www.beckers hospitalreview.com/pdfs/hospital-review/June_2011_HR.pdf

Pettigrew, A., L. McKee, and E. Ferlie. (1988). Understanding Change in the NHS. *Public Administration Public Administration* 66(3): 297–317.

Pinchot, G., III. (1985). *Intrapreneuring.* New York: Harper & Row.

Pirsig, R. M. (1974). *Zen and the Art of Motorcycle Maintenance: An Inquiry into Values.* New York: Morrow.

Pollack, A. (2011, July 29). Ruling Upholds Gene Patent in Cancer Test. New York Times. http://www.nytimes.com/2011/07/30/business/gene-patent-in-cancer-test-upheld-by-appeals-panel.html

Pollock, A. (2004). *NHS plc: The Privatisation of Our Health Care.* London: Verso Books.

Porter, M. (1980). *Competitive Strategy.* New York: Free Press.

Porter, M. (2010, December 23). What Is Value in Health Care? *New England Journal of Medicine* 363: 2477–2481.

Porter, M., and E. Teisberg. (2004, June). Redefining Competition in Health Care. *Harvard Business Review* 82(6): 64–76.

Porter, M., and E. Teisberg. (2006). Redefining Health Care: Creating Value-Based Competition on Results. Watertown, MA: *Harvard Business Press.*

Porter, M., and E. Teisberg. (2007, March 14). How Physicians Can Change the Future of Health Care. *JAMA* 297(10): 1103–1111.

Reay, T., W. Berta, and M. Kohn. (2009). What's the Evidence on Evidence-Based Management? *Academy of Management Perspectives* 23(4): 5–18.

Robbins, J. (1996). *Reclaiming Our Health: Exploding the Medical Myth and Embracing the Source of True Healing.* Tiburon, CA: Kramer.

References

Rowe, J. (2008). *The Parallel Economy of the Commons.* State of the World 2008. http://jonathanrowe.org/the-parallel-economy-of-the-commons

Sarpel, U., C. Divino, B. Vladeck, and P. Klotman. (2008). Fact and Fiction: Debunking Myths in the US Healthcare System. *Annals of Surgery* 247(4): 563–569.

Selznick, P. (1957) *Leadership in Administration: A Sociological Interpretation.* Evanston, IL: Row, Peterson.

Sen, A. (1999). *Development as Freedom.* New York: Knopf.

Sengupta, S. (2007, April 5). A Bangladeshi Army of Housewives Battles Tuberculosis. *New York Times.* http://www.nytimes.com/2007/04/05/world/asia/05iht-bangla.1.5156156.html?

Servan-Schreiber, D. (2008, September 19). We Can Stop the Cancer Epidemic. *New York Times.* http://www.nytimes.com/2008/09/19/opinion/19iht-edservan.1.16308287.html

Shapero, A. (1977, February). What Management Says and What Managers Do. *IN-TERFACES* 7(2).

Sibley, D. (1995). The Hyperthyroid Economy. *Journal of the Royal Society of Medicine* 88(6): 305.

Simon, H. A. (1950). Administrative Behaviour. *Australian Journal of Public Administration* 9(1): 241–245.

Smecher, C. (2007, Autumn). Complete Solutions: How Communities Can Work Within and Around the Established Health System. *Making Waves* 18(3): 7–11.

Smith, J., K. Walshe, and D. Hunter. (2001). The "Redisorganisation" of the NHS. *British Medical Journal* 323(7324): 1262–1263.

Spencer, F. (1976, November). Deductive Reasoning in the Lifelong Continuing Education of a Cardiovascular Surgeon. *Archives of Surgery* 111(11): 1177–1183.

Strom, S. (2012, July 7). Has "Organic" Been Oversized? *New York Times.* http://www.nytimes.com/2012/07/08/business/organic-food-purists-worry-about-big-companies-influence.html

Systems Leadership Steering Group. (2016, February 3). *The Revolution Will Be Improvised.* London: NHS England. http://www.thinklocalactpersonal.org.uk/_assets/News/The_Revolution_will_be_improvised_Part_II.pdf

Taylor, D., Jr. (2002). What Price For-Profit Hospitals? *Canadian Medical Association Journal = journal de l'Association medicale canadienne* 166(11): 1418–1419.

Taylor, F. (1911). *The Principles of Scientific Management.* New York: Harper.

Tierney, J. (2009, September 21). To Explain Longevity Gap, Look Past

Health System. *New York Times.* http://www.nytimes.com/2009/09/22/science/22tier.html

Tuohy, C. (2007, June 19). *Competition and Collaboration in the English Health Reforms.* Presentation for the Nuffield Trust.

Vaill, P. (1989). *Managing as a Performing Art: New Ideas for a World of Chaotic Change.* San Franciso: Jossey-Bass.

Verghese, A. (2011, September). *A Doctor's Touch.* TEDx talk in Montreal. https://www.ted.com/talks/abraham_verghese_a_doctor_s_touch/transcript

Wachter, R. (2016, January 16). How Measurement Fails Doctors and Teachers. *New York Times Sunday Review.* http://www.nytimes.com/2016/01/17/opinion/sunday/how-measurement-fails-doctors-and-teachers.html

Welch, H. (2008, October 7). Preventive Medicine or Overdiagnosis? *New York Times.* http://www.nytimes.com/2008/10/09/health/09iht-snmyth.1.16748310.html

Wikipedia. (2016). Fractal. http://en.wikipedia.org/wiki/Fractal

Woolhandler, S., T. Campbell, and D. Himmelstein. (2003). Costs of Health Care Administration in the United States and Canada. *New England Journal of Medicine* 349(8): 768–775.

Woolhandler, S., and D. Himmelstein. (1999). When Money Is the Mission: The High Costs of Investor-Owned Care. *New England Journal of Medicine* 341(6): 444–446.

World Health Report. (1999) *Making a Difference.* Geneva: World Health Organization. http://www.who.int/whr/1999/en/

World Health Report. (2000). *Health Systems: Improving Performance.* Geneva: World Health Organization. http://www.who.int/whr/2000/en/

Zaleznik, A. (1977). Managers and Leaders: Are They Different? *Harvard Business Review* 55(3): 67–78.

Zaleznik, A. (2004, January). Managers and Leaders: Are They Different? [Reprint] *Harvard Business Review* 82(1): 74–81.

Zitner, D., and D. Kelderman. (2007). A Third Way Forward: Canada's Communities Can, Should & Must Intervene in Health Care Delivery. *Making Waves* 18(3): 2–6.

INDEX

Index

Index

Index

Index

Index

Index

Index

Index

Index

Symphony orchestra study, 33–34, 70, 156
Synergy, 213
System of health care, 6, 147
  bridging relationships in, 229–230
  cooperative autonomy in, 233
  as failure, 9, 15–21
  health activists in, 232–233
  health navigator in, 230–232
  information and knowledge in, 221–224, 232
  myth of, 2, 11–13
  reframing of, 213–233
  with single payer, 226–229
  as success, 16–17
  synergy in, 213

Taber, P. G., 81
Taylor, D., 104
Taylor, F. W., 153
Taylorism, 32n
Technocratic politicians, 61
Teisberg, E., 31n, 42, 51, 52n, 53
  on business of health care, 88
  on competition, 60, 64, 78–80, 83n, 83–84, 86
  on government role in health care, 100n, 100–101
  on measurement and calculation, 160
  Redefining Health Care, 53, 80
  on strategy, 175n
Telephone triage, 70n
Thiel, P., 82n
Tierney, J., 76n
Time and motion studies, 88, 153
Top management, 35–36, 143
  reframing of, 169–171
Tracking Strategies (Mintzberg), 175n
Transformational leadership, 27, 170n
Treatment of disease, 125
  compared to focus on prevention, 11–13, 86, 118, 122, 215
  cost of, 17–18
  success in, 16
Trudeau, P., 61
Tuohy, C., 41

United States, health care in
  business of, 87, 89, 92–93
  compared to Canada, 76, 100n, 101–102, 228, 228n
  competition in, 75–86
  cost of, 18, 72, 76, 76n, 84–85, 93, 100, 109n, 184
  failure of, 15
  malpractice lawsuits in, 78n
  Medicare in, 19n, 91n, 228
  outcome of, 76
  plural sector, 102–103
  and preventable death rate, 76
  private insurance model in, 102n
  in Veterans Administration, 26, 44n, 82n, 101, 102
Users of health care, 117, 118
  separation from providers, 139–142

Vaill, P., 131
Value-based competition, 31n
Veterans Administration, 26, 82n, 101, 102
  information technology system in, 44n, 82n
  scale of, 44n
Vocabulary of health care, 147, 152, 225
  reframing of, 219–220

Wachter, R., 62
Walls, 2, 116, 127, 142
Warwick, W., 55–60, 63, 64, 66, 142, 159, 160, 175
Watson, J., 81, 82
Wellness, map of, 122, 124
Who Killed Health Care? (Herzlinger), 88
Wikipedia, 106–107, 178, 179, 220, 233
Wong, T., 38, 38n, 39
World Health Organization, 15, 47, 76n, 141, 203
World Health Report (1999), 16

Zaleznik, A., 24
Zen and the Art of Motorcycle Maintenance (Pirsig), 71
Zitner, D., 37n

259

THE AUTHOR
AND THE OTHERS

ABOUT THE AUTHOR

I am Cleghorn Professor of Management Studies at McGill University in Montreal, where I have spent most of my career since receiving my doctorate from the MIT Sloan School of Management in 1968. In 2006, I helped found the International Masters for Health Leadership (imhl.org) to change not only management education for health care, but also the practice of health care itself, by bringing into an ongoing forum mid-career managers and professionals from all aspects of the field worldwide. I continue active teaching in this program, alongside a similar one for managers from business (impm.org), and supervise doctoral students at McGill. I am also a founding partner of CoachingOurselves.com, which enables teams of managers—many in health care—to develop themselves and their organizations in their own workplaces.

This is my 18th book, and my 5th with Berrett-Koehler. (*Managers not MBAs* was published in 2004, *Managing* in 2009, *Simply Managing* in 2013, and *Rebalancing Society* in 2015.)

Since 2014, I have been writing a regular TWOG (tweet2blog: @mintzberg141 to mintzberg.org/blog) as "provocative fun in a page or 2 beyond pithy pronouncements in a sentence or 2." (Examples: "Managing scrambled eggs," "Confronting socially transmitted epidemics," "Has the Berlin Wall fallen on us?") In 1997, I was elected an Officer of the Order of Canada and in 2015 received the Lifetime Achievement Award from Thinkers 50. Twenty universities around the world have granted me honorary degrees.

Most important, I continue to spend my public life dealing with organizations and my private life escaping from them—in a canoe, on a bicycle, atop skates, and up mountains, alongside my wonderful partner, daughters, and now sometimes three grandchildren as well.

ABOUT THE PEOPLE BEHIND THE AUTHOR

Many people can contribute mightily to a book whose authorship seems so personal. For this one, I have to single out for special appreciation Mary Plawutsky, and earlier Ariane McCabe, who contributed a great deal to the preparation of this manuscript. My special thanks as well to colleagues who commented on recent or earlier versions of the manuscript (which spanned a decade): especially Sheila Damon, but also Abe Fuks, Rafael Bengoa, Gordon Best, Sholom Glouberman, Ted Marmor, John Breitner, and Brenda Zimmerman. Kristen Herzegh and Marie Leinberger made special contributions as reviewers. Leslie Breitner now runs the IMHL wonderfully well, which has contributed so much to this book. Thank you to all the great graduates for so many ideas. Earlier Diane Marie Plante contributed significantly to getting the program started, and therefore to this book as well.

Beyond this book, after I gave a talk at the University of Salerno in 2010 about the myths, my host, Paola Adinolfi, teamed up with her colleague Elio Borgonovi to do an edited volume. They asked a number of prominent scholars and practitioners in Italy and elsewhere in Europe to write commentaries on each of the myths. It is being published at almost the same time as this, by Springer, under the title *What Is Right and What Is Wrong in Health Care Management? Commenting on Henry Mintzberg's Myths*. They did not have my book—they used an earlier article I did based on it (Mintzberg, 2012), nor did I have a chance to see theirs before I finished this one, but the two together should prove to be interesting.

Berrett-Koehler remains a treasure of a publisher. Its special Author's Day enabled us to sit down with the entire staff to discuss the book. And quite remarkably, among that staff, Steve Piersanti, founder and president, provided the most detailed comments.

Santa Balanca-Rodrigues has been rendering my professional life smooth and fun for 20 years. This has probably helped to take years off this book, while adding them to my private life. And happy I am for that, because, on the personal side, Dulcie Naimer brings a warmth and a love that I can express best by dedicating this book to her.

To Dulcie,
source of so much of my health and happiness

Berrett–Koehler
Publishers

Berrett-Koehler is an independent publisher dedicated to an ambitious mission: *Connecting people and ideas to create a world that works for all.*

We believe that the solutions to the world's problems will come from all of us, working at all levels: in our organizations, in our society, and in our own lives. Our BK Business books help people make their organizations more humane, democratic, diverse, and effective (we don't think there's any contradiction there). Our BK Currents books offer pathways to creating a more just, equitable, and sustainable society. Our BK Life books help people create positive change in their lives and align their personal practices with their aspirations for a better world.

All of our books are designed to bring people seeking positive change together around the ideas that empower them to see and shape the world in a new way.

And we strive to practice what we preach. At the core of our approach is Stewardship, a deep sense of responsibility to administer the company for the benefit of all of our stakeholder groups including authors, customers, employees, investors, service providers, and the communities and environment around us. Everything we do is built around this and our other key values of quality, partnership, inclusion, and sustainability.

This is why we are both a B-Corporation and a California Benefit Corporation—a certification and a for-profit legal status that require us to adhere to the highest standards for corporate, social, and environmental performance.

We are grateful to our readers, authors, and other friends of the company who consider themselves to be part of the BK Community. We hope that you, too, will join us in our mission.

A BK Business Book

We hope you enjoy this BK Business book. BK Business books pioneer new leadership and management practices and socially responsible approaches to business. They are designed to provide you with groundbreaking and practical tools to transform your work and organizations while upholding the triple bottom line of people, planet, and profits. High-five!

To find out more, visit **www.bkconnection.com**.

Berrett–Koehler
Publishers

Connecting people and ideas
to create a world that works for all

Dear Reader,

Thank you for picking up this book and joining our worldwide community of Berrett-Koehler readers. We share ideas that bring positive change into people's lives, organizations, and society.

To welcome you, we'd like to offer you a free e-book. You can pick from among twelve of our bestselling books by entering the promotional code **BKP92E** here: http://www.bkconnection.com/welcome.

When you claim your free e-book, we'll also send you a copy of our e-newsletter, the *BK Communiqué*. Although you're free to unsubscribe, there are many benefits to sticking around. In every issue of our newsletter you'll find

- A free e-book
- Tips from famous authors
- Discounts on spotlight titles
- Hilarious insider publishing news
- A chance to win a prize for answering a riddle

Best of all, our readers tell us, "Your newsletter is the only one I actually read." So claim your gift today, and please stay in touch!

Sincerely,

Charlotte Ashlock
Steward of the BK Website

Questions? Comments? Contact me at bkcommunity@bkpub.com.

Certified

Corporation
bcorporation.net